Jennie Dean
c.1852–1913

UNDAUNTED FAITH...

The Life Story of
JENNIE DEAN

Missionary, Teacher, Crusader, Builder.
Founder of the
MANASSAS INDUSTRIAL SCHOOL

by

STEPHEN JOHNSON LEWIS

Memorial Edition

The Manassas Museum gratefully acknowledges the financial support of IBM Corporation which made the reprinting of UNDAUNTED FAITH possible.

Published by
The Manassas Museum
Manassas, Virginia 22110

Copyright 1994

ISBN: 1-886826-04-8

Typography by REF Typesetting & Publishing, Inc.
Manassas, Virginia 22110

Printed by BookCrafters, Inc.
Fredericksburg, Virginia 22404

Printed in the U.S.A.

Table of Contents

Introduction vii
Douglas K. Harvey, Museum Director

Acknowledgements ix

Foreword to the Memorial Edition xi
Brig. Gen. Clara L. Adams-Ender, U.S.A., Retired

Undaunted Faith 1
Dr. Stephen Johnson Lewis

Historic Photographs 92

Epilogue 121
Laura A. Peake, Museum Specialist
Scott H. Harris, Museum Curator

Index 131

Bibliography 141

**Manassas Industrial School/
Jennie Dean Memorial Donors** 145

Introduction

When I came to The Manassas Museum in 1982, members of the community quickly made me aware of the inspiring story of Miss Jennie Dean and the school she founded. There were also two aging paperback copies of the book *Undaunted Faith* in the Museum collection. From these sources, it became obvious that there was a notable history involving the Manassas Industrial School and its founder that was little known to the general public.

Dr. Stephen Johnson Lewis was a dentist in Manassas who had benefitted from an educational beginning at the Industrial School. Dr. Lewis determined that a biography should be written as a tribute to Miss Dean and as an object lesson to the youth of that day. Dr. Lewis felt that Jennie Dean had never been given credit for the selfless contributions she had made to better "her people."

Undaunted Faith was printed in a very limited edition by The Circuit Press in Catlett, Virginia in 1942 and was sponsored by the Northern Virginia Baptist Association. While the number of volumes in the original printing is unknown, there must have been relatively few given the number of surviving copies. The Library of Congress determined that the book had not been reprinted since 1942 and the copyright had expired, thus making this reprint possible.

In 1989, the Manassas City Council approved a project to build a memorial honoring Miss Jennie Dean. The Memorial will be built on the original campus of the Manassas Industrial School. As a corollary to these efforts, the Museum desired to reprint *Undaunted Faith*. The synergy of reprinting the book as part of the Memorial process became obvious to all and grant funds for both were sought.

It was especially fortuitous that IBM saw value in these projects for in 1992, the company awarded a $40,000 grant with $25,000 earmarked for the Memorial and the balance to reprint *Undaunted Faith*. With this generous grant, planning for the reprint began in earnest.

It was decided that the original book would be reprinted faithfully with only typographical errors corrected. This was done to preserve the flavor and feeling of Dr. Lewis's original work. However, many unpublished historic photographs had been added to the Museum collection as well as early school catalogs, oral histories, and other materials not available for the original book.

The Manassas Historical Committee and Museum staff decided that the appropriate method would be to add these into an expanded Memorial Edition of *Undaunted Faith*. By this method, the story of the Memorial, donor lists, a history of the school since 1942, and a bibliography could be added to aid the future scholar and interested reader.

General Clara Adams-Ender graciously agreed to prepare the new forward to *Undaunted Faith* while still Commander of Fort Belvoir, Virginia. She also enthusiastically endorsed the Memorial project as the memorable keynote speaker at the September, 1993 project kickoff. Though separated by years and circumstances, General Adams-Ender and Jennie Dean are linked in their commitment to community service, education and personal achievement.

It is our sincere hope that this Memorial Edition follows the tenet lived by Miss Dean and noted by Dr. Lewis--that faith makes all things possible. The Museum is grateful to all those who helped this book and the Memorial become a reality and it is our pleasure to make this story of courageous achievement available to many new readers.

Douglas K. Harvey, Director
The Manassas Museum System
October 1994

The Family of Stephen Johnson Lewis wishes to express their appreciation to all those whose efforts produced this new edition of *Undaunted Faith*.

We are certain that "Uncle Steve" would be pleased that his work will continue to honor the memory of Miss Jennie Dean by sharing her inspiring story with a new generation.

Diane M. Lewis
October 1994

The Manassas Museum wishes to thank
the following individuals and groups
for their contributions to
UNDAUNTED FAITH: THE MEMORIAL EDITION

City of Manassas

Manassas Historical Committee

Manassas Museum Associates

Manassas Society for the Preservation of Black Heritage

IBM Corporation

The Library of Virginia

Gloria Bennett-Jones	Jennie Dean Club
Louise Smith Brown	James Knox
Dr. Judith Saunders Burton	The Family of Stephen Johnson Lewis
Edward Coleman	Elizabeth Nickens
Rosa Farquhar	Dr. J. Harold Nickens, MD
Anna E. Ferguson-Corbett	James H. Payne
Evelyn Fields	B. Oswald Robinson
Clara and Russell Fincham	Charles Smith
Frances Gary	Dorothy Smith
Hilda and Garland Hicks	Dr. William Waddell, DVM

Foreword

"A woman whose sacrifices and vision matched well with those of Douglass, Lincoln, and Booker T. Washington." This is how author Stephen Johnson Lewis described Miss Jennie Dean in his original introduction to her biography, *Undaunted Faith*, in 1942. And what a remarkable and visionary woman she was! Born into slavery in Northern Virginia in 1852, Jennie Dean received almost no formal education. She possessed no great powers of oratory, friends in high places, or family connections.

How could this black woman of the 19th century with no discernible strengths engage the rich and powerful of her day? How did she plan and create the Manassas Industrial School for Colored Youth which opened in 1894 and taught thousands of minorities who had no other access to education? Why is a memorial to Jennie Dean and the school she founded so important today?

Jane Serepta Dean was a woman with purity of vision. When slavery ended in 1865, she was all of 13 years old. The world she had known in western Prince William County was shattered in both the physical and societal sense as the old plantations were desolate and destroyed. The fences were gone, the crops were gone–even the trees were gone after years of camp fires and cannonades. The old ways of life were also gone. There were no masters and no slaves but also no schools, no money, and no jobs. In the midst of desolation and upheaval, however, was the strong new power of freedom.

Seeing opportunity where others saw only chaos and obstacles, Jennie traveled the 30 miles to Washington seeking work and a new life. Unlike many other blacks who left their former homes, Jennie maintained a strong linkage to her native Northern Virginia. Working as a domestic in the

Nation's Capital, she returned home on weekends to train "her people" in life skills, to establish churches, and to ultimately create her masterpiece: the Manassas Industrial School.

With purity of purpose, with great vision and energy, Jennie Dean traveled to New York, Boston, and Philadelphia seeking those who could help with her life's mission and work. Because of her profound belief in education and service to others, Andrew Carnegie, Oswald Garrison Villard, and the lesser-known Hackleys and Howlands all provided large donations for buildings and operations at her school. The people of Northern Virginia also heeded her call with donations to the school from former slaves, former Union soldiers, and former Confederates. The coalition of people who supported Jennie Dean and the school may be viewed through those attending the dedication in 1894: Clara Barton, Frederick Douglass, former Confederate General Eppa Hunton, and Edward Everett Hale.

Jennie Dean's path was not always easy in the administration of the school. There were fires, conflicts with boards and principals, and ill health with which to contend. Indeed, there was a time when Jennie Dean was ostracized from the school she had founded, shunned by the administrators. However, her love for people, her belief in education, and the school she founded endured even after her death in 1913.

What is the legacy of Jennie Dean? In simple terms, it is the belief that with the Creator's help all things are possible. The accomplishments of Jennie Dean in the face of adversity can be a lesson for us all. There are always evils in the world and we can always give in to fear of war, AIDS, inflation, racism, and to fear itself. But there are those who walk through this world with a greatness and a power not to be denied, and Jennie Dean was one of those people. She was visionary, self-directed, determined and persistent. The legacy and significant accomplishments of this magnificent heroine and genuine human being shall stand the test of time and history.

> Brig. Gen. Clara Adams-Ender
> U.S.A. Retired

Foreword

**Brigadier General
Clara L. Adams-Ender
(Ret.)
Former Deputy Commanding General,
Military District of Washington
and
Commanding General, Fort Belvoir**

Brigadier General Clara L. Adams-Ender was born in Wake County, North Carolina and received her baccalaureate degree in nursing from North Carolina Agricultural and Technical State University, Greensboro, North Carolina. She later received a Master of Science Degree in Nursing from the University of Minnesota, Minneapolis, Minnesota; and a Master of Military Art and Science Degree from the U.S. Army Command and General Staff College, Fort Leaven-worth, Kansas.

A veteran of over 30 years in the Army, General Adams-Ender has held such diverse assignments as Chief Nurse of two medical centers, Assistant Professor of Nursing, Inspector General, and Chief Army Nurse Recruiter. Her overseas assignments include Korea and Germany, where she served as an Intensive Care Nurse, REFORGER Chief Nurse, Medical Center Chief Nurse, and Nursing Consultant.

For three years, General Adams-Ender served as Chief, Department of Nursing, Walter Reed Army Medical Center, Washington, D.C., the largest health care facility in the DOD. Awards and decorations include the Distinguished Service Medal, Legion of Merit, the Meritorious Service Medal with three Oak Leaf Clusters, the army Commendation Medal, the coveted Surgeon General's "A" professional designator for excellence in nursing administration, the Roy Wilkins Meritorious Service Award of the NAACP, and membership in the Order of Military Medical Merit.

In 1967, General Adams-Ender became the first female in the U.S. Army to qualify for and be awarded the Expert Field Medical Badge. In 1980, she became the first and only nurse and female to be senior marcher for 700 U.S. Army Europe soldiers in the 100 mile, four-day march in Nijmegen, Holland. In 1987, she became the eighteenth Chief of the Army Nurse Corps, and in 1988, she became the first Army Nurse Officer to be appointed as Director of Personnel for the Surgeon General of the Army.

General Adams-Ender is a member of the Association of the United States Army, the American Nurses Association, the National League for Nursing, the American Organization of Nurse Executives, Sigma Theta Tau, International Honor Society, Delta Sigma Theta Sorority and Chi Eta Phi Nursing Sorority. She retired from active duty in September, 1993.

FIRST EDITION

Published by
"THE CIRCUIT" PRESS
Catlett, Virginia – August 1942

* * *

Sponsored by
The Northern Virginia Baptist Asssociation

COPYRIGHT AUGUST 1942 by
STEPHEN JOHNSON LEWIS
Manassas, Virginia

The Cover design [previous page] is the work of Mr. George W. Robinson a native son of Manassas, an alumnus–now resident in New York City. This and the plate for the design, is the joint contribution of Mr. Robinson and Mr. Edward R. Martin, both of whom received their secondary training at Manassas Industrial School.

[Editor's Note: The original printing plate for the cover of *Undaunted Faith* is in the collection of The Manassas Museum.]

Contents

	Preface	xix
	Acknowledgements	xxi
	Introduction	xxiii
I.	Introductory Chapter	1
II.	Birth and Childhood	5
III.	A Comparison	9
IV.	Building a Background for Industrial Training	13
V.	A Dream Becomes a Reality	17
VI.	The Beginning of The Manassas Industrial School	21
VII.	Jennie Dean Speaks	23
VIII.	Growth of The School	29
IX.	First Tragedy	33
X.	The Beginning of a New Era In The School's Progress	37
XI.	More of The School She Founded Than of Jennie Dean	41
XII.	The School Chartered, Began Its Work In 1894	43
XIII.	The Little Oak Begins Its Fight For Maturity	49
XIV.	Some of The Early Characters	53
XV.	The Waning Influence of Miss Dean	55
XVI.	An Era of Trial and Balance	59
XVII.	Not Dead But Sleepeth	65
XVIII.	Attempt For State Aid or Control	67
XIX.	The Parade Increases Its Tempo	73
XX.	Regime of Dudley Saw The School At Its Lowest Ebb	79
XXI.	The Parade of Principals Temporarily Ends	83
XXII.	The School Today As A Regional High	87
XXIII.	How Well She Builded and With What Results	89

[Editor's Note: The pagination of this Table of Contents differs from the original due to its incorporation into the Memorial Edition.]

DEDICATED TO THE MEMORY

of

Landonia Randolph Lewis, My Mother, whose
almost entire life was associated with that
of Miss Dean and her work

* * *

Elizabeth Howard Lewis, My Wife, who ever
encouraged my interest in the School and
who early suggested my writing the
life story of Jennie Dean

* * *

The Rev. William James Howard, My Father-
in-Law, who for nearly twenty years was
a trustee of the School and one of its
most loyal supporters.

* * *

Preface

Much of the basic material involved in the following biographical sketch and narrative, lay unused and largely unappreciated for its storied worth, in my files, until the death of Miss Dean. Through my family relationship and connection with the School and even with the subject of our sketch during all of her matured life, much material was thus available. Upon the passing of Miss Dean, it occurred to me that this material offered the foundation for a commendable story. I began to seek for other material, meeting with only slight interest from those who had worked with this crusading missionary.

More than five years ago, following my return to Virginia and re-association with the School she founded, as an active working alumnus I decided to correlate my data and put it in story form. Many of those formerly available, had passed on. This did not deter me and upon the urging of an alumnus, a lifelong friend, I determined to pass on to the youth of Northern Virginia the life story of a woman whose sacrifices and vision matched well with those of Douglass, Lincoln, and Booker T. Washington. By this time, perhaps I had more fully acquired some of the real art of narration. At least my friend, Edward R. Martin, felt that way. And here is the story.

In presenting it, I have as my main objective the stimulation of the youth of my group in this Northern Virginia area, to lives of greater achievement as a tribute to the woman who gave her ALL for them. I have called the story "UNDAUNTED FAITH" for if Jennie Dean possessed any quality above all others, it was faith in her plans and objectives. Faith in her power to make better the living conditions of her people and to save its youth from lives of wanton lust, idleness, degredation and servility to the influence of poverty.

In the introduction of this volume, Dr. Brooks speaks of Jennie Dean as "A Woman of God, Unafraid." This surely typifies her real character. She believed in herself and in the unfailing power of prayer in overcoming obstacles and in the meeting all of her problems. She was a Disciple of Christ unusually endowed and though an uneducated woman in terms of schooling, Miss Dean possessed a wonderful vision, a capacity for planning and a technic for winning friends to her causes and then making them succeed, which it seems many of our collegiates do not even approach.

Thus I feel that these impressions of our subject are sufficient to warrant the time and energy I have spent in putting the story of her life in print.

Through the fine cooperation of the Moderator and officials of the Northern Virginia Baptist Association itself, in assembly, through the agency of the Circuit Printing Company, publication and distribution is made possible. It is the author's hope that this book as a storied memorial to Jennie Dean, may prove a tribute of high worth to the region she served.

STEPHEN J. LEWIS, D.D.S.
Manassas, Virginia
August 1942

Acknowledgements

The writer desires to express his full appreciation to the following persons and groups who so willingly cooperated in the gathering of material and data for this story by personal interviews, loan of records and correspondence, opening of their personal files for inspection and for the moral encouragement of others; all of which meant so much in carrying the task to completion. Without this material and moral aid, the job could not have been done:

Mr. Edward R. Martin of Brooklyn, New York, a native son of Manassas, graduate of the School (classmate) and for many years a trustee, whose faith in my ability and continuous moral urge kept me at the task until completed and but for whom I possibly would have not completed it.

Mr. Oswald Garrison Villard of New York City, whose part in the story is definitely cited; for his words of encouragement and willing cooperation.

Mr. John W. White and Dr. J.D. Williams locally for permission to examine voluminous files and the loan of data.

Rev. William H. Barnes, present Principal of the School, for access to the institution's files and the loan of official data and records.

Prof. Edward D. Howe, Principal of the Booker Washington High School, Suffolk, Va., for his fine spirit of cooperation and the loan of his files.

Dr. Leslie Pinckney Hill, Principal of Cheney Teachers College, Cheney, Pa., for preparation of data and other assistance given.

Prof. William C. Taylor, Principal of Rosenwald High School, Warrenton, Va., for many interviews and much data and information given.

Mr. Richard C. Haydon, Superintendent of Prince William County Schools, for data and information furnished.

Miss Eva P. Lewis, formerly nurse in charge of Berwind Hospital, for priceless data she had preserved and willingly loaned.

Mrs. Annie B. Rose, niece of Miss Jennie Dean, for material loaned.

Mrs. L.L. Marshall, of Culpeper and Mrs. Katie Williams of Manassas, old friends of Miss Jennie Dean and who gave so freely of their memories of her and her activities. And to the host of others who gave interviews and whose names are not all recorded or recalled, I offer my heartiest thanks and appreciation.

Finally, to Rev. Frank E. Hearns, for many years Assistant in the Columbus Memorial Library of the Pan American Union and Moderator of the Northern Virginia Baptist Association, and officers of the Association as well as the Association as a whole, I offer additional thanks for the fine spirit of cooperation evidenced in officially offering to sponsor the publication of this story and to manage its distribution in the Northern Virginia area. Thus, to all who have cooperated with me in any degree whatever, I am deeply thankful.

(Author)

Introduction

Of the many requests for advice, comment and help during the more than half a century of my ministry, requests for aid in similar writing projects etc., I can think of none which brought more genuine interest and pleasure than that of the biographer of Miss Jennie Dean, who asked me for a foreword or introduction to this splendid portrayal of the life of a splendid woman.

Like the writer, I congratulate myself that I was a part of the spiritual life of Miss Jennie Dean over a period of years covering most of her mature life. She became a member of the church I have pastored so long, in her early teens, being baptized on profession of faith and received as a member of the Nineteenth Street Baptist Church, Washington, D.C., in the year of 1866 as the record shows.

I am thoroughly familiar with much of her early life during the years of her missionary work in the Northern Virginia area, when as the author has so well told us, she was laying the foundation stones for a life of genuine usefulness in the organizing of Sunday Schools and the building of missions and chapels many of which remain today in active service as established churches. During these days, she came to me often for advice and counsel and I found a deep and supporting interest, not only in these earlier projects but later, in the School itself.

I have mentioned that Miss Jennie Dean became a member of my church in 1866 when she was just fourteen years old, according to the birth records shown in the story. Thus she came to Washington as a mere youth, likely in search of employment and possible advancement from her former rural life. She, like many other Negro youth of the time, was caught in the migratory movement of that period and which even now, still goes on. As 1865 marked the close of the Civil War and the legal extermination of the institution of human slavery in America, there were millions of ex-slaves, poor beyond measure, homeless and without means of support, thousands of whom followed the Federal troops to be fed and cared for by them. Others flocked to nearby hamlets, towns and cities, while bolder souls made their presence known in the far North.

Jennie Dean thus came to Washington, the capital of the Nation, seeking work. What she sought, she found and in so doing found friends for herself and for "her people"; friends of influence and means; friends of the highest order of intelligence and many of whom had the philanthropic spirit. Friends who had the time and patience to listen to her story of interest in others, of whom she thought more than of herself.

Accordingly, when the opportunity came, she returned to the area of her birth where she had conceived the vision of actual need and then went far and near, on horseback or in her little old sulky, planting Sunday Schools and otherwise laboring to make Christ known and to teach His Gospel to the youth wherever she would get them together. Thus we have a constructive interpretation of the Master, "Seek ye first the Kingdom of God and His Righteousness."

But in her spiritual zeal she did not forget the physical needs of her people. To meet these needs, she gave to her native State and to her racial group, the Manassas Industrial School, an institution planned by her as a blessing to the body, mind and spirit of these folk she so much loved. The men of her day might well have said, "O Woman, great is thy faith."

Should such a woman, born in slavery, deprived of anything but the very rudiments of an education; a woman who dedicated her whole life to self-sacrifice for her people and her God, be forgotten? Dr. Stephen J. Lewis, whom she seems to have spiritually adopted as a mere child, answers that question in giving to her world and its public at large, his excellent story of Jennie Dean's life and work.

I commend it and urge both racial groups of Northern Virginia which she served so well, and others who are genuinely interested in real human interest stories, to read the story and note the hand of God in giving to humanity His precious blessings through the work and sacrifice of this one woman of the lowly of His flock.

> WALTER H. BROOKS
> Pastor of Nineteenth Street
> Baptist Church
> Washington, D.C.
> October 25, 1941

I
Introductory Chapter

JUST how long I knew the character who is the Subject of the story I now begin, is wrapped up in the uncertainties of youthful memories. That she visited my farm home many times prior to the incidents hereinafter related, is unquestionably true. As the youngest of my family of six children–and where there were children, "Miss Jennie" was always a visitor–and because of my extreme youth at that period, it is likely that I received more attention from our visitor than my elders of the family and because of her mothering instincts the impressions she made upon my youthful mind were perhaps more lasting.

Thus it is more than likely, and in fact is substantiated by living members of my family, that she had been a regular visitor to our home many years before the outstanding incident which seemed to impress her indelibly upon my mind as a child. I could not have been more than seven or eight years old and I recall that I was then regularly attending Manly School, walking three or more miles to and fro daily.

It was one of these periodic week-end visits during the course of her community rounds as a religious missionary and civic worker that she spent Saturday night in our home. On Sunday morning she told my mother that she wished to take me with her in the sulky, a one seated, two wheeled vehicle pulled by the ever faithful and well known bay mare Chaney–to Sunday School. I knew that Sunday School was being conducted in the same building in which I had attended day school but my memory is that I had never been permitted to attend Sunday School with other children. I recall how my mother assented and how filled with youthful joy I became.

The ride behind Chaney in the little old sulky, whose single seat was almost completely occupied by "Miss Jennie" herself, was but a minor part of the excitement in this new childish experience and all or even a minor part of the details are wrapped up in the mists of a rather remote past and would have no direct bearing upon this story if remembered. But characteristic of events and incidents brought from our youth through the medium of the mind's storehouse, many of which seem stamped there for future reference and use, this one incident coupled with another I shall later relate, stands out vividly as my first youthful impression of constructiveness of my storied heroine.

The Little Red School House–and it was actually painted red, its admixture of benches for the tots and discarded desks and seats which had outlived their usefulness in the white schools, but easily identified in this respect by the knife-carved initials of more than one generation of former users who seemed to have left but little space for the carving of our own; the mixed group of Sunday School attendants and the element of expectancy involved, all left definite impressions. But outstanding in these mixed impressions on my youthful mind were those made or created by the teacher, the superintendent, the guide, the mentor and the mother of this group, all characteristics identified in a single personality, "Miss Jennie."

I was thus early introduced formally if we shall call it that, to a personality who had in all probability held me in her arms as a baby and who was to become, in the years to follow, a definite factor in the moulding of my moral and religious concepts as a growing youth and as a direct aide to my mother and who was later to figure definitely in my secondary education a personality stamping herself upon my youth with impressions never to be erased.

Thus with this brief primary background of a relationship as a starting point, coupled with a direct and indirect association with her for nearly a half century and until her earthly career was finished, I feel justified in trying to set to record a summarized biographical sketch of her life and because of these early impressions and later associations with her, I feel in a degree qualified as her biographer. In addition I feel in duty bound to make available to the Negro youth of Northern Virginia the salient points of her career of service as a fitting inspirational background upon which they may build constructively in her memory.

Thus in brief retrospect, I present a partial background upon which I hope to weave a story with Jennie S. Dean of Sudley Springs, Virginia, as the central figure. Hers will be the leading role for it is about her that I chiefly write. It is a story of a woman born within the meshes of slavery, of slave parents and during the last years when slavery was legal bondage; a woman who grew to maturity physically, minus a striking personality or what might be called a magnetic, winning smile. She was not endowed with beauty as we call it. She was very dark; almost black and distinctly negroid in features with no evidence of inherent Aryan physical traces easily discernable.

No artist would have denominated Jennie Dean ugly, for there was a beauty and simplicity of expression in her face which bespoke sternness of character and definiteness of purpose. Her piercing eyes while void of vulgar boldness, were always attuned to a definite focus and totally void of that nervous hesitation and swaying sweep as characteristic of folk in a state of uncertainty. There was no cringe in her manner of approach, even to notables whom she met. Thus there was so much of genuine beauty in her social bearing (her chin ever up) so much of impressive simplicity and directness that she created impressions more because of these striking elements than any other.

I write of a woman who seemingly was endowed in her early years with a life purpose of personal sacrifice and service to a selected cause and who gave to "Her People" of Northern Virginia so much more than she ever received. It is a narrative of activities begun and confined to a limited field of action chosen by her, a field to which she dedicated her entire mature life. It is of an influence which spread far and wide in its national scope because of this unique dedication to a single purpose, born unquestionably of a spiritual endowment in which the missionary spirit was predominant.

II
Birth and Childhood

MISS JENNIE was born near Sudley Springs, Va., in the year of 1852. There is no available record of the day and month. She was named Jennie S. Dean, just what the S. stands for I am unable to learn, but to all of the various communities of Northern Virginia in which she labored, she was known simply as "Miss Jennie." *[Ed. note: Jennie Dean's full name was Jane Serepta Dean. The date of her birth is not confirmed. Numerous sources suggest she was born in 1852. One death certificate indicates she was born April 15, 1848 (information supplied by her sister Ella Dean Bailey). A second death certificate filed for her suggests she was born in 1853. Early 20th century census records indicate she may have been born as late as 1860, however that seems unlikely.]* Her father was Charles Dean and her mother, Annie Dean. There were two sisters, Mrs. Ella Dean Bailey, and Mrs. Mary Dean Martin, one brother, Charles Dean and a half brother, Henry Bennet. Her grandmother was named Mildred and was said to have been an Indian woman of mixed blood. Ruben was her grandfather. Her parents were owned in slavery by the Cushing and Newman families. It is related that at her birth, an old Aunt Aimee, observing that she was born with one tooth erupted, observed: "This is going to become a real woman some day."

Her childhood background is best related in an article written and published by Oswald Garrison Villard, who in his paper, *The New York Evening Post,* figures so prominently in this story later on. In this article, Mr. Villard outlined the background of the Manassas Industrial School which she founded: "The story of the building of the Manassas Industrial School is almost the life story of Jennie Dean. Her father and mother were slaves but were of the most intelligent class of Negroes, the father having been taught to read and write in early life. After the War he settled down on a farm near Sudley Springs, Virginia on the actual battle-ground of Bull Run. It was his ambition to own this farm but he died before the purchase was completed.

Jennie Dean, then a well grown girl, went into service in Washington, her wages going to pay the balance remaining on the farm, that her mother might be assured of a home." Thus her only opportunity for an education was what she could glean in a few months only from the then very primitive public schools provided for colored folk. Hence it would not be unwise to presume that her basic education did not, to a very large degree, exceed that attained by her father who unquestionably was of the house-servant class of slaves in that he was taught to read and write.

Much space could be devoted to many related incidents of her childhood if so much of it were not mere hearsay, and many also of her early matured years which very forcibly affirm the missionary spirit which was hers but the limited nature of this storied sketch will not permit. Here I might state that one of my critics observed that I was losing a "biographical opportunity" in not relating more of Miss Jennie Dean's childhood and by those who knew her as a child. This "opportunity" is fully realized, but the absence of living relatives who might furnish the items so much desired makes my reference to Mr. Villard's hearsay evidence as reliable as is otherwise available.

However; additional quotations from Mr. Villard's *Evening Post* article shed the necessary light on her youthful ambitions and activities: "Later her wages were used to send a younger sister to Wayland Seminary from which she was graduated and became a public school teacher." Here I interupt Mr. Villard to add that this sister later married a minister of prominence in the county of her birth, Rev. L.H. Bailey. This sister, through the growing influence of Jennie Dean at this time, together with her husband, became factors in the religious and civic life of Northern Virginia and both served on the trustee board of the School Miss Dean founded. But back to Mr. Villard. "Her life in Washington at length opened Jennie Dean's eyes to the needs as well as the possibilities of her people. Her thoughts were continually with 'my people at home,' and her mind was tortured with dreams and plans of helping them. Her first work was the founding of a Sunday School."

To speak in common parlance, here at the conclusion of Mr. Villard's last sentence in this quotation, we might "stick a pin" for in the establishment of this first Sunday School as a mere girl missionary, she set up the first milestone of a career during which she most capably demonstrated her ability as an organizer through her unusual ability to win friends to the many causes she represented and the many undertakings she fostered and mastered.

The childhood years of Jennie Dean are wrapped up in the same elements of obscurity as were those of Lincoln, Douglass, and Booker T. Washington. While there are those yet living who recall that her parents, as Mr. Villard has already told us, were not of the ordinary type of their time and conditions and that her home life was probably conducive to clean living, yet knowing the restrictions placed upon impoverished parents in those years, it is safe to assume that to a very large degree Jennie Dean, like the proverbial "Topsy" "just growed up." These parents were known as upright, aspiring, thrifty, and honorable citizens who, out of a life of bondage in slavery, had undoubtedly learned much and experienced more than they desired their offspring to learn or experience. We do know that there was little time or means of giving this ambitious girl the attention she deserved or perhaps not sufficient intelligence for them to realize her capabilities.

It is safe to say, however, in their behalf, that by sheer comparison with their own lives and ambitions they had inspired the child to profit by her freedom of body and mind and "Make something of yourself." This, it seems, was the primary admonition of folk of the time to their children. Deeply religious, no doubt, as were most colored folk just out of bondage, they unquestionably leaned heavily on prayer and their religious devotion in the guidance of their children. We do know that these humble folk built up a philosophy of life out of their trials and tribulations in slavery which re-echo in the spirituals now recognized as America's only original folk songs. And is there any finer philosophy extant?

These admonitions involved are plain and simple, but all-inclusive in the tenets of the more scholarly treatises bearing on youth and their outlook. There was another basic admonition which parents like hers always gave: "Be polite to the white folks." We of today would modify this admonition to include all folk, but these slave born folk had learned all too well the need of specific instructions because they knew well the virtue of catering to the good-will, charity, and favor of those possessed with the power to hurt, hinder, harm, or help. This was not necessarily teaching humility or servility as we are now prone to interpret it, but rather was meant to fortify the youth of the time against the evils and pitfalls of arrogance and incivility in the face of unsurmountable barriers.

Thus Jennie Dean must have learned these lessons well, for the story of her later life proves how well she nurtured these principles, and how well they served her in her life's most constructive accomplishments.

These same parents gave to our subject another characteristic of which they were perhaps not wholly aware (and yet who knows but what they did actually teach these principles to her) that education is not necessarily schooling in formal sense but is available wherever you will take it, whatever its nature–in good or evil, harmful or hurtful, filled with virtue and constructiveness or stuffed with fraud and chicanery.

This child of theirs seems to have had the faculty of absorbing the best from those with whom she came in contact and weaving the lessons learned into a sort of personal philosophy embodying wit and wisdom, tolerance, courtesy, self-control and determination. These inherent virtues as character foundation-stones, developed later into diplomacy and poise which gave to her that personality which in later life was to win for her so many worthwhile and useful friends from both racial groups. Friends whose names and deeds and loyalty are indelibly a part of her life story.

III

A Comparison

ON a recent Sunday morning I listened to the radio program, "Wings Over Jordan." Charlotte Hawkins Brown was the speaker and her theme was "Social Graces and the Negro." Her plea seemed to be that in a correct development of good manners each toward the other, or in discriminating between the good and the bad in human relationships, socially and culturally, we are laying the foundation upon which a constructive and useful life may be built; the cultivation of these primary virtues in human society which mean so much in the proper development of our youth and their harmonious progress in life and in this very complex state of "American civilization."

When I reflected upon the rare social graces and cultural attitudes so keenly evident in that group of our colored ancestry, and of our orthodox parents still living today, who absorbed these social and cultural virtues as domestic servants in the homes of the upper classes (sometimes called the aristocracy) of the South, particularly in post Civil War days, and then transmitting, as it were, these virtues to their offspring when they were susceptible to such influences, I could but recall the voice of Jennie Dean diligently preaching this same doctrine in her simple words nearly half a century ago.

Charlotte Hawkins Brown of North Carolina and Mary McLeod Bethune of Florida are but improved types of Jennie Dean of Northern Virginia who pioneered here in this section along almost identical lines in teaching these fundamentals to social and economic progress, before either of them had begun the training which was to give them the advantage of more competent implements.

I referred to my files and found therein a pamphlet written by Jennie Dean in 1896 and entitled "Jennie Dean's Rules for Good Behavior Among her People." I could think of no better place to use this item of material than in assigning it here, as it seemed to be echoed down through the years in the choice language of a more modern Jennie Dean, whose background is much the same but whose education and training fits her well for the job she is doing for "Her People." She, like Mrs. Bethune and Booker T. Washington, firmly believed in the development of those primary qualities of humility of soul as Christian virtues applicable to both God and man and the cultivation of those simple but important virtue of politeness, good manners and how to win the favor of those in authority through the medium of correct social and cultural attitudes in daily relationships.

In this pamphlet of Miss Jennie Dean's admonitions we find such simple cautions as "Politeness Home and Abroad"; "Don't be Late in Going to Church." Such other items as "If You Are Late, Take the Seat Nearest the Door," "Seat Your Company First," "Don't Turn Your Back To the Speaker," "Don't Address an Audience With Your Hands in Your Pockets," and she might have added "Don't Sit in the Aisle Seat and Have All Other Comers Scramble Over You to be Seated." Admonitions on attending funerals, street conduct, travel conduct, home relationships, table etiquette, on visiting girls, in general public company, etc.

This pamphlet with its many admonitions on social conduct was distributed by Miss Jennie Dean with the same social objectives nearly fifty years ago as those of the radio broadcast of this scholarly lady who is in a large degree, a modern counterpart of our own Jennie Dean. Truth is fundamental and remains unchanged through the Ages. One must first learn how to obey politely, and with it the art of courteous serving if he would know how to rule or be served. A real leader has been a good follower. To serve willingly and well is to fit one's self to be served and to be gracious in receiving that service as when giving it.

Jennie Dean had these virtues. They seem to have been a part of the very fibre of her physical, mental and moral makeup. Gifted with a keen mind and observation and well defined powers of discrimination plus a deep religious devotion, had she belonged to a later generation there is little doubt but that she would have graced the pulpit, for she was the preacher of the unemotional type and a crusader for righteousness. Fortunately this was not to be her role for in it she would have lost much of the opportunity for the type of service to which she fell heir and in which she so well acquitted herself. She might have evangelized the masses but likely would have lost the opportunity to influence the individual lives of the youth of her time, so many of whom she started towards lives of constructive living and progress.

IV

Building a Background for Industrial Training

TO further quote Mr. Villard's *Evening Post* story: "For two consecutive summers these Sunday School meetings were held at her home and at the end of that period she began to talk to the young men and women of the desirability of holding together during winter and of ultimately building a church." The recital in brief tells the story of the extreme poverty of the people of the community and how the system of exchange or barter was the chief method of doing business because little money exchanged hands.

However, this leader began at once to seek a site for the proposed church and finding the desired location which the owner agreed to sell on easy terms of payment. "Even the small amount he demanded appalled the people." Here Jennie Dean first showed her mastery as a leader and organizer in being ready with a plan of action which these folk could understand. As Mr. Villard put it, she substantially said, "you can each give something if only a day's work. Whenever you sell something, lay aside a small sum, if only a few pennies, for the building fund. Those who have nothing to sell, come and give your labor when we raise the building. After my day's work is done, I will go out and try to collect money for the fund."

In a comparatively short time the church was built and flourished for many years as both a place for worship, Sunday School and as a primitive community center under the name of Calvary Chapel. Other missions and Sunday Schools followed in neighboring communities and with old Chaney, the ever faithful bay mare, she moved from community to community on her rounds of conducting services, holding Sunday School sessions, building both family and community morale and truly evangelizing Northern Virginia or that part of it she could cover in the "Horse and Buggy Days" but ever dreaming and working towards that larger goal of establishing a school for industrial or vocational (as we now know it) training of the youth of her group. Many of the missions she established became organized churches under her influence, among them being Prosperity Chapel in Loudoun County, Catharpin or Calvary, Dean-Divers Chapel all becoming churches and many other smaller missions which survived for a long period.

In connection with her Sunday School work, she held Saturday afternoon classes in cooking and sewing, bringing to the community folk the benefit of her experience as a domestic during the winter months she had spent in service in Washington. She was much influenced by these industrial classes and turned her thoughts to the real need of expanding the idea to a more practical application as a means of better preparing these young folk for lives of usefulness. What Tuskegee and Hampton had accomplished according to the stories she had read about them, undoubtedly spurred Jennie Dean to real action.

Let Mr. Villard again tell the culmination of these dreams and ambitions through the newspaper article: "It was after twelve years of mission work that she first decided to devote herself to the industrial education of the Negroes of Northern Virginia. She realized the evils which resulted from the exodus of hundreds of her Sunday School scholars to the city slums and alleys but she also realized the hopelessness of their fate when they remained at home. She remembered the skilled labor of many of the men and women trained in slavery, and while rejoicing that her people were free, she regretted that nothing had ever arisen to take the place of the industrial side of slavery." That something should be done about it was the soul-possessing problem facing Jennie Dean at this important stage of her career and that she decided to DO SOMETHING about it, and how, is told in the chapters following.

Building a Background

Hackley Hall

V
A Dream Becomes a Reality

IN the opening paragraphs of this story it was related how I gained my first impression of "Miss Jennie" through my first trip to one of her many Sunday School missions. Now I turn to the second and more lasting impression she made upon me and it is perhaps an inbred tendency because my mother figures so prominently in it. And it does seem sort of parallel that since my life interest in her has to do largely with the institution she established, the part it played in my career-foundation and my years of association with the institution and with her as its founder and moral director for many years of its existence, that this early impression I am about to relate had to do with the School itself.

    I was young enough to be still fond of my mother's lap and it was there I nestled on this winter evening during one of "Miss Jennie's" week-end visits on her Sunday School tour of the region. We sat before the open fire-place and I vividly recall how she told my mother of the school she planned and that a Miss Thompson offered to secure a site for it near Thoroughfare Gap. My mother, as I learned later in life, was intensely practical and she asked Miss Dean why she would think of establishing a school in so remote a section. She urged her to come nearer to Manassas Junction in seeking a location, for this being the junction of the Southern Railway main line with its Strasburg Branch and the transportation and shopping center of this section at this time. After much conversation on the subject of location and the school proposition in general, I recall my mother suggesting she knew of a farm which could be secured and the next day as I have heard Mother relate many times since, she drove Miss Dean to the Hampton Brenton Farm (now the site of the School) to look it over and ascertain if he would sell it for the purpose desired.

I cite this second youthful impression of "Miss Jennie," not in a desire to claim any distinction for my mother because of the incident, and I know it to be true, but rather because out of my youth there seems few incidents occurring around my age then, which are recalled more vividly than the two first impressions of "Miss Jennie." I call this second-memory-incident singularly linked with the first, because no one gave more actual and moral support to Miss Dean during those pioneer days than did my mother and because my family has been closely identified with the institution from its founding. I personally graduated from its third class in 1900, served as a trustee from 1921 to 1924 and may be counted to this day one of the most ardent alumni and citizen supporters.

Since there is no story, impartially written, which gives a keener insight into the early life of Miss Dean and her ideals and ambitions—surely none of the material I have been collecting over the last few years in preparation for this sketch—than the story of Mr. Villard, already quoted from, I again let him speak to you of the events leading up to the founding of her monumental work for "Her People." Quote: "Her influence had grown very strong in the community and the people received with confidence anything she said to them. She called a number of them together and said: 'Keep your children at home. Don't send them to the cities. You must buy your lands; become taxpayers. Make all you can. Meanwhile, I will go out and raise the money to build a school where your children can be educated to trades. You do your part and I will do mine out in the world.'"

This quotation from Mr. Villard, printed in the catalog of the School in 1912, seems to portray the character and determination as well as the life purpose of Miss Dean better than any hearsay or recorded word she ever uttered. YOU DO YOUR PART AND I'LL DO MINE was the philosophy of a life of sacrifice in which she asked only reasonable moral support and belief in her to the extent of

A Dream Becomes a Reality

making that faith tangible with a constructive contribution of some sort–whether moral or material. In return, she gave HER ALL in her every undertaking, whether in relieving distress in some family of her area of action, establishing a Sunday School or mission, laying plans for a church or chapel where it seemed a community need or in this larger field of planned action, giving industrial training to the boys and girls who so much needed it.

VI

"The Beginning of the Manassas Industrial School"

THE title of this chapter is written by Miss Dean herself and much of its context is her recital of this "beginning" as she gave it in her pamphlet entitled "The Beginning of The Manassas Industrial School For Colored Youth And Its Growth," and published in 1900 (the year of my graduation from the School).

The foregoing chapters tell the story of how she prepared herself in securing definite and first hand knowledge of the needs of "Her People" through her early years in religious and social work in the various communities which were later to become the supply source of the School itself. Today we would call her procedure a "social survey" with all the necessary and complicated technic involved, but to Jennie Dean, in these early years, it was simply "getting at the bottom of things" and trying to do something about it.

The Bull Run battle area which had known the clash of men and arms just a few decades before in the struggle which freed "Her People" from physical slavery, was to become a new battle front in a much different sort of "Campaign of Manassas" in another attempt for a constructive freedom–mental and economic freedom.

Jennie Dean did not begin this "Third Battle of Manassas" with forces disorganized as many at that time seemed to think in their attitude of discouragement. When they asked her the provincial question, "Where in the world are you going to get the money from?", she had an answer in "You Do Your Part," and again "The Lord will provide a way."

Her "general staff" consisted of a host of friends she had made and advised with for many years in her mission work and they were not confined to the Virginia area of action. She had many staunch friends and counsellors all throughout the East and in New England and New York City, which were then the centers of national philanthropy. Her first-line campaigners were local colored and white friends she knew she could depend upon in the initial stages of her drive and they were, for the most part, folk she could call neighbors. Back of this first-line organization stood this fine group of stalwart reserves who were only waiting action to win for her, through them, other worthwhile friends and supporters about whom she tells you in her own story to follow.

VII

Jennie Dean Speaks

SHE tells the story in her own simple words much better than any biographer could. Therefore, I let Miss Dean, herself, speak: "I have been often asked about the origin and growth of the Manassas Colored Industrial School, situated at Manassas, Virginia. Having been engaged in organizing and reorganizing four Sabbath Schools, I found through this work many boys and girls who would be smart in more ways than one if they had an opportunity. I began to think what could be done for them. I planned in mind for a long time. At length, one October morning a farmer called to see me about his children as he had seven sons and wanted them to have trades. I told him he must pray over the matter and God would open the way somehow.

"Time passed on and at length one cold January morning in 1888, my mother, Rev. D.G. Henderson, and I were sitting by a log fire talking over the conditions and welfare of the young colored people. I then told them what Mr. Shellington had said about his seven sons and also what I had in mind, what kind of schools we needed, the teachers, and how to get food and other necessary things to begin with. All would have to give the first year's work free, as we were all poor. In the same year, my sister, Ella Dean, who worked in the Sunday Schools with me, was appointed teacher for the public school at Thoroughfare Gap.

"There was a Southern lady there by the name of Miss Jennie E. Thompson, and the work of the industrial school was talked over again; there was a large number of colored people in and near this place; some had served Miss

Thompson's parents in the days of slavery. It is true that she was young and knew nothing of the past and yet her eyes were open and her heart tender towards the needs of the young people in the way of proper training, education and trades. Miss Thompson said that money she had not, but she would do all in her power to help find friends who had money or controlled it, and who would help us in that direction.

"We thought at first to have the school at Thoroughfare Gap, but we soon found that it was not the proper place for it. I called on Rev. M.D. Williams of Manassas, Va., and Rev. L.H. Bailey (her brother-in-law) of Occoquan, Va., and told them what we women had in mind and they said we needed such a school and that they would publish it from their pulpits, but where the money was to come from was the problem. We began to appoint committees in different neighborhoods and most of our white friends promised to do what they could, while some gave me cold words, but as the Apostle Paul says, 'None of these things moved me,' for my mind was made up and I went right on. I always remembered my father's saying that 'True Friends are the old ones.' I knew that the friends that I had made when I was in the Congregational Bible Missions School were not all dead and as they had so kindly helped in my first work, which was building chapels for Sunday Schools, I believed they would help again in this work.

"Our first public meeting was called at Manassas in November 1890. After the school had been discussed, Mr. John Johnson called our attention to a beautiful farm owned by a Mr. Brenton which he carried thirty of us to see." (I interrupt Miss Dean here to refer again to my "second lasting impression" of her in the before related story of my mother's calling this farm site to her attention in my home, whether before or after this related visit by the group to the said farm–but certain verifying local proofs would seem to indicate that it was well before the visit). Miss Dean continues: "We were all delighted with it. When asked the price, he said he wanted $2,650.00 for it and $100.00 cash in a few days to bind the bargain. The farm is located at the Junction and we all knew that it was a fine place for a school. We then had only $60.00 in the bank, which I had collected while working in Marion, Mass.

"Miss Thompson came from Washington for the meeting and on her return called Mr. H.E. Baker's attention to the work we had started, and he kindly lent us $40.00 to make up the $100.00 so we could be safe for a while. The committee that was appointed to see that the money was properly paid was composed of Rev. M.D. Williams, Mr. George C. Round and Mr. John Johnson, all of Manassas as we had not yet gotten to the place to have trustees. We had to get the work well planned before we went too far. One of the first things was to see how many colored people were in the five adjoining counties near Manassas. We soon found there were 23,972 and over 11,000 of school age.

"We had a number of meetings to see which persons were best suited to serve as trustees, and to get someone who would undertake to get $1,400.00 to meet the first payment on the land. At every meeting someone was ready to go, until the time came, and then the ones who were ready and willing came up missing and the lot fell on me.

"I talked with Dr. Clarkson (superintendent of schools in Prince William County), Capt. Tyler of Haymarket, 'Squire' Cushing of Catharpin, Virginia, and Judge Gaines of Warrenton, and they gave their endorsement. Congressman Meredith of Manassas, Va., kindly wrote friends of New York and I found them very kind–they contributed very generously to the work. Among others, I saw Prof. H.P. Montgomery and Gen. Eaton of Washington, D.C. These gentlemen endorsed the work and promised they would do all in their power to make it a success. I called on Dr. B.P.M. King of Washington, President of Wayland Seminary. He gave me my first dollar of the $1400.00. I also called on Dr. Rankin of the Howard University and Dr. Newman of the First Congregational Church, also Hon. John M. Langston. Miss Thompson had found friends in Boston and other cities who had promised to assist in the work.

"The first ones who acted as a Board of Managers were Gen. Mussey, president, Prof. H.P. Montgomery, vice president, Miss J.E. Thompson, secretary, and Mr. H.E. Baker of Washington, treasurer. We had only begun the work a few months before the hand of death removed Gen. Mussey. Dr. R.R. Shippens, his pastor, filled his place. I arrived in

Boston January 8, 1891. My first meeting was held on the 9th, and the collection was $3.00. Nearly everyone said I had come at a bad time, for the banks were the question of the day in Boston. When I left Washington I had only $9.00, outside of my ticket, for my personal needs. It is true that I had walked many miles to save five cents, but still my money went, for I had to have a place to stay and something to eat. I began to wonder what was the best thing to do, for I was determined to save every penny that had to be given to the school. I then remembered a lady by the name of Mrs. Wilcox who had so kindly helped me in building a chapel at Conklin, Va., when I was at Boston a few years before. With some little trouble, I found her at 15 Holyoke Street. I told her of my errand in Boston and that I was willing to do anything to save room rent and board and she kindly gave me employment.

"In the midst of the names given me by Miss Thompson were Dr. Edward Everett Hale and Mrs. M.C. Whitman of Boston. Dr. Hale is a gentleman who the world seems to have a claim on, yet he was not too busy to give some of his time to the work of Manassas. Mrs. M.C. Whitman kindly accepted the office as treasurer for Boston. When I found they had so kindly lent a hand, I felt as if I was straight for the work. Among the letters I had there was one to Bishop Brooks who was always ready to give a kind word to the needy, and who gave the first $30.00 in Boston and promised when the land was paid for, he would help us to build, but before that time came, he left earth for Heaven.

"Dr. J.M. Savage, who then had a large church in Boston, gave me my first $75.00. I had not gone the space of two months before I was taken sick. Col. Dudley and wife kindly took me to their home and cared for me until I was able to work again.

"Mrs. Whitman and Dr. Hale were securing appointments for me and had quite a number by the time I was well. Dr. A.J. Gordon of Clarendon Street Baptist Church and Dr. Gordon of Old South Church also secured me appointments. When there was $940.00 in the treasury, two ladies called one day and gave me $61.00 and they were never heard from anymore.

"The reader can imagine how thankful I was to the

Lord and kind friends when I found we had the first one thousand dollars to pay on the land. I toiled until we had $1400.00. In October 1891, Rev. M.D. Williams and his people at Manassas, gave a five cent reception and raised over $70.00. Mrs. Whitman of Boston was present at the reception. This was her first visit and she picked out the site for the first building. Early in the winter of 1892 the women's attention of different neighborhoods was called to decide about having a fourth of July dinner. To make this a success we started early.

"The committees appointed in different neighborhoods were: Bull Run, Mrs. F. Harris; Conklin, Mrs. F. Douglas; Sudley Springs, Mrs. G. Berry; Wellington, Mrs. Landonia Lewis (the writer's mother); Gainesville, Mrs. Susan Barber; Manassas, Mrs. M.D. Williams. On the Fouth, the committees and friends from far and near came; some in lumber wagons, ox teams, walking and on the trains, bringing baskets with old fashioned pound cakes, fried chicken, bread, pies and many different things to suit the taste. We had three different priced tables–ten cents, twenty-five cents and fifty cents. We had speaking and singing and by three o'clock the dinner was all over and we had cleared $75.00. From the first dinner the people were all enthused and the work grew wider and wider.

"When the time came to get ready to build, the men's attention was called to the work on the land. Free day's work was appointed for teams and laborers. Some of them had to come eight and ten miles. Teams from Bull Run were Anthony Harris, Bladen Robinson, Tasker Robinson and John Free. Wellington, William Lewis (the writer's father), Wm. Griffin, Mrs. Sallie Stokes and Wm. Jackson. Sudley Springs, Nelson Elliott, John Peters, Mrs. Charles Dean and John Shellington. Men and teams from Manassas, John Green, David Washington, Mrs. Martha Chapman, John Johnson and Henry Berry.

"Each vicinity had different dates. The first day among the workers, was a dear old brother by the name of Henry Gilliam (writer's grand-uncle Henry Gilliam) between 75 and 80 years old. He said he could not read, as his young days were spent in slavery–and the tears ran down his aged face, thanking God that he could help in this work for his neighbor's children. Through Mrs. Langhorne of Virginia, in February 1893, an opportunity was given me to present the work before the Women's Suffrage Convention which was in session in Washington. There I met Miss Emily Howland of Sherwood, N.Y. I soon found that she was a friend of the work. She visited the farm and liked it. She said as it was the work of women that she would give $1000.00 to finish paying for the farm, which she did, and helped to build when we were ready,. The building was soon started and in September 1894 the beautiful Howland Hall was dedicated with appropriate exercises.

"A beautiful flag was given by Miss Jennie E. Thompson. When we raised it, it floated once to the breeze and then collapsed. Some said that it was a token of trouble. Rev. Bradford of Washington, D.C., led in singing the hymn 'My Country Tis of Thee.' An audience of about 1500 persons, old and young, joined in the singing. Prayer was offered by Rev. Creditt then of Washington, D.C., after which there was speaking by the Hon. Frederick Douglass, Dr. H.M. Clarkson, Capt. Tyler and others."

VIII

The Growth of the School

THE foregoing quotations from Miss Dean's own story of "The Work" and its progress and given to the reader in her own language, portray well the devotion and personal sacrifices involved in first awakening the local folk to the need for the school and secondly in organizing them for action and then winning to the cause such a large array of worthwhile and prominent folk of the other racial group. But Miss Dean glazed over much of the difficulty she had in keeping her local forces intact and it shows the sterling qualities in her character when these items, many of which were most disheartening, are not even referred to in her own story. However, there is this to say; Many of the local characters who were prominently identified with her in the beginning, showed difference of opinion as to her procedure. There was the forming of factional groups pitted each against the other; the struggle for local leadership in the various sections of the community of action under her generalship, all of which is most natural and not an unexpected thing in any large movement involving so many folk and personalities. As a result, however, many worthy names were omitted from her biographical sketch, names which represented much in both moral and material support in those trying early days. Her story is highly colored with the names of those who, at the time of her writing, favored her most and whom she most admired, and particularly those with whom she had had no disagreement on policies and procedures.

Rev. L.L. Marshall and wife, of Culpeper, Va., (his name being casually mentioned as a trustee or director) were among the most active of her early advisors and supporters and although they advocated the Thoroughfare Gap site for the school, they joined in full support of the project when Manassas was selected. Mrs. M.D. Williams and my mother, Mrs. Landonia Lewis, were also only casually mentioned, although their support and influence is a matter of record from the days of mere talk without action and then on into the formative days and through the years without interruption until the one passed to reward, while the other lives in the memories of a life identified with the institution through her influence and activity; her husband's life-work for the school and her son's taking up the task upon the occasion of his father's death.

These two latter families have been identified with the school since its founding, and since Miss Dean's passing, and through their progeny have, and still are, an intimate part of its local setup and present status as a Regional High School. These families are mentioned as examples merely and because of their continuous and outstanding loyalty, but they by no means complete the list of the many names of local folk not mentioned by Miss Dean, but who were and still are, through their progeny, continuous chains of support and influence.

But back to Miss Dean's story of the "Growth of the School." "In October of 1894, school opened in the dwelling house (the farm house which became Charter Cottage later) as Howland Hall had not been completed. There were six pupils to open with but the number soon increased to seventy-five. Prof. H.P. Montgomery acted as principal until Dr. E.P. Clemons and wife came to take charge of the school. The faculty comprised of Dr. Clemons, principal; Mr. Jefferson Thomas, teacher in carpentry; Mrs. Clemons, sewing teacher; Miss Mary E. Vernon, cooking teacher, matron, housekeeper and literary teacher. These instructors gave free their first year of work receiving only their board in return.

Howland Hall was soon completed and there were seventy-five young people in it for study. Many things were needed in the building and on the farm. We needed wood, furniture, books, wagons, cows, etc. Sunday Schools, churches and friends donated to the school. Barrels of flour

The Growth of the School

and corn were given by white friends of Sudley Springs and Catharpin: Dr. C.F. Brower, 'Squire' Cushing, Mr. F.H. Sanders, Mr. Metcalfe, Mr. J.D. Polen, Mr. L.I. Anderson, Mr. Henry Ayers and Mr. Thomas Patman. The Mt. Calvary Church (Sudley Springs), pastor Rev. D. J. Henderson, and its members and friends, gave chickens, meat and vegetables. The 'Prosperity' church at Conklin, pastor Rev. L.H. Bailey, members and friends donated the same. The Bull Run church, Elder Bell, pastor, congregation and friends gave wheat and corn."

And so on and on the list of willing donors of various items is cited by Miss Dean. These donations may be summarized for space to include everything from pigs to smoked ham in barrel; tools for both shops and farm and furniture for Howland Hall's many rooms.

IX

First Tragedy

THEN let Miss Dean tell of the "first great tragedy." "In the fall of 1894, I went to Boston again for the school. I stayed there until January 1, 1895, then came to New York with many letters of endorsement from prominent people to the same in New York, one of the most prominent being Rev. Grant, D.D. I found him quite friendly to the work and he told me that I should meet the ladies of his church. Before I returned to see Dr. Grant the sad news came that the beautiful Howland Hall and contents had been reduced to ashes by the dreadful monster fire, turning seventy-five students and teachers out of doors, shelterless and without clothes. They had only the pleasure of using the building about four months. One can imagine our feelings after having such a struggle to get it. We have met the same disaster all through the six years of the school's existence. We can never recover our losses in these buildings.

"Through the energy of Prof. H.P. Montgomery and the kindness of friends, the school lost but little time after the burning of Howland Hall. There was a small church near, which was neither lathed nor plastered, so they tacked up blankets and quilts to keep the severe cold of February and March out and held school there the remainder of the term until we rebuilt. He said he was willing. He gave the first $100.00 on rebuilding. Rev. Greer, D.D. gave $200.00. Rev. Williams, D.D. of All Souls Church; Rev. Huntington, D.D. of Grace Church, N.Y., Bishop Potter and Rev. Collier, D.D. (who sympathized with me, as he had lost his church by fire) all stood by the work and helped me make it a success."

Then Miss Dean tells of the contributions of Mrs. Burton Harrison who helped to raise $2000.00 and who became treasurer for New York, assisted by Mrs. Judge Howland. Howland Hall was soon rebuilt with the additional association of such names as she relates: Mr. H.P. Dodge and friends of Manassas, Mrs. H.P. Montgomery, Miss M.B. Cook of Alexandria; Rev. H.H. Waring (who later became an official of the School), Rev. Elliot of Boston and the ladies of Dr. Hale's and Dr. Gordon's churches, all contributing cash or furniture or cooking utensils or clothing, linen, etc. Thus with this temporary setback, the "work" again went forward.

Let Miss Dean again speak: "I went to New York in January 1896. Mrs. L.A. Hale sent me to see Mrs. C.B. Hackley who had been a faithful friend. At this time we did not have a separate building for the boys. When she knew this, she willingly had one built at the cost of $3000.00 and furnished it with the assistance of Mrs. L.A. Darling of New York. It bears the name of Hackley Hall, (the writer worked as a lather on this building during its completion–for tuition). The boys were delighted to have such a building. Through the carelessness of the contractor not doing his work according to agreement in reference to furnace and pipes, on January 25, 1900, I heard screams. When I looked, lovely Hackley Hall was on fire. We worked hard and saved most of the things but if my heart had not been made of something more enduring than steel, it would have broken. No one but God knows how it affected me.

"How to face the people of New York and Boston was a hard problem to solve but something had to be done. Trusting in God and believing He would be with me, I started in October 1900, to Boston and New York again, to walk the streets in the cold, pleading the cause of the School before the past and present friends. They never said to me "No," but with sympathy, were ready to come to our assistance. Mrs. C.B. Hackley was ready to assist notwithstanding that $3000.00 or more had been lost in the burning of the building. Through her generous gifts and other friends we have another building erected. The teachers and students raised the first money for the rebuilding of Hackley Hall which is now a lovely brick building for boys and will be dedicated November 5, 1901, while Howland Hall is the girls' building. We thank God for such good friends, praying and trusting that blessings may ever abide with them, that we may have no more such losses as we have had by fire."

The concluding paragraphs of Miss Dean's sketch book tells of the school as it then stood; established, operating successfully with two splendid buildings, then purged as it were by fire which took both of them and as if by a Divine plan, rebuilt and moving forward. Fourteen buidings as she puts it had been erected by this date "Large and small" to use her language, "all paid for except Hackely Hall." She cites the nine branches of industry under the supervision of eight instructors with two-thirds of the farm under cultivation. She tells further, of the establishing of the blacksmith and wheelwright department through the kindness of Mrs. L.A. Hale of New York and Miss Osgood of Boston, and the equipping of the laundry by Mrs. L.A. Darling "who also gave useful things for the girls' rooms and gave presents as Christmas gifts."

Organization of Women's clubs in behalf of "The Work" is related and many names associated with it, which space will not permit listing. At the close of her story, she tells of the teachers in charge at that time as Prof. E.H. Woodford, Berea College, Kentucky, Principal; Assistant principal John W. White, of Washington, D.C. High School; Cooking and assistant in literary branches, Miss Mary E. Vernon, Washington High School; and trained in Mrs. Bancroft Davis' Cooking School (D.C.), Sewing and literary branches and Matron, Miss Bessie E. Loving, Howard University; Carpenter teacher, Mr. Samuel W. Johnson, Hampton Institute; Laundry teacher, Mrs. Josephine Thompson, Manassas, Va.; Blacksmithing and wheelwrighting, Mr. Roscoe C. Lewis, Hampton Institute and of the Lewis family of Manassas.

I now let Miss Dean have the concluding words of her autobiographical sketch: "During our six years of work we are thankful to say, through the assistance of God and kindness of good friends, our school has done well. During our work we have been able to turn out thirty girls as seamstresses and sixteen teachers. The girls teach sewing along with their English in school."

X

The Beginning of a New Era in the School's Progress

THE preceding chapters which are terminated with the story of "Her Work" by Miss Dean herself, covers as well as the writer is able to do so with available material and from his own personal knowledge and that of the many persons who knew her and were associated with her throughout her life of the activities enumerated, or at some time during the period covered. The story thus far depicts, or aims to, the preparatory stages in her life for the ultimate establishment of a practical and permanent agency of help to "Her People"–The Manassas Industrial School.

Allowing for the normal variations and vicissitudes which are a part of any life or movement involving so many people, communities, conditions of life and primary problems to be solved, the life of Miss Dean up to this point and the things she had accomplished, must have been a source of much satisfaction to her. She had overcome many difficulties in reaching the present goal; had built an influence in her field of action; had won to her cause and causes a host of friends from all walks of life and including some of the most outstanding and most worthwhile Americans then in public life.

With the endorsement of such outstanding national characters as Edward Everett Hale and Phillip Brooks with their wide circle of contacts and influence in the field of charity and philanthropy, Jennie Dean had reached the point in her life as a missionary with a high purpose, which gave no need for mere introduction to the Nation's best folk. The School with its background of struggle and sacrifice was now established as an institution with promise of continuous service and sustenance. The picture to her must have had a rosy hue. But true to the comparison with the variations of human life, not far ahead lay many obstacles to be overcome, many acute problems to be solved and many heartaches for our heroine which included almost complete banishment from participation in her project by the new group which ultimately came into control of it. With the dawn of a new century, a new phase of her life began and from the position of a respected "Mother Superior," founder and moral supervisor of the institution, she was to be relegated to the sidelines as a mere wishful observer with perhaps a temporarily blighted spirit but a still undaunted determination. Sentimentalism it seems, was on the wane and hard realism had entered the picture as the institution became a living and growing organism.

As an organizer of "The Work" in initiating the movement for the establishment of the school and as a harvester of friends and supporters, she had perhaps reached the peak of her real usefulness. As administrator in the role of sort of "Mother Superior," she was not equal to the task she perhaps still felt was hers in helping to shape the policies and procedures in the management and planning for the future of the school. The incorporation of the institution brought to the fore men of keen business vision and experience and it is likely that with them she clashed.

There are on record some very unfortunate situations which on the surface seem to many to have involved unfair treatment of her, bordering on sheer disrespect for the sacrificial work she had done and her high objectives. However, it is not for the biographer to enter judgment on who was at fault or the real causes underlying these seeming misunderstandings. It may have been a clash of personalities, over-ambition on the part of some and lack of vision on the part of others. There may have been flaws in the "foundation" which some realized and wished to correct before further building. This, Miss Dean might have resented. I do not know. In this process of evolution from a rather crude beginning, as meritorious as this beginning was–these apparent differences in opinions involving possible future policies were not at all unnatural and these temporary flaws perhaps constitute more the element of success built on failure or the "ups and downs" of life than any deliberate attempt to discount the merit of her work and accomplishments. However as her biographer, I count this period as the era of temporary shadows and even after her passing, these shadowy periods were intensified or become more numerous and were not as I see it, the direct result of the attitude or actions of any one individual. It is unfortunate, however, that these shadows enshrouding Miss Dean at this time, were not wholly dissipated before her passing.

XI

More of the School She Founded Than of Jennie Dean

THE preceding chapters relate much more of the personal life of Jennie Dean than of any one outstanding thing she accomplished. Elaboration upon her origin, her self-developed missionary program, her sincere devotion to bettering the conditions of life among her people and particularly to improving and making newer and more constructive opportunities for the youth of her group and her final decision that an institution must be established to that end, have been as fully narrated as the space will permit. Page upon page could be added in a minute recital of many untold items which would surely add color to this story but are neither expedient nor necessary to present it to the youth and the public of Northern Virginia. It is a record of unselfish devotion to an adopted plan of life which embodied genuine service to the cause she advocated, almost total elimination of self in that devotion and of the accomplishments wrought.

Beginning now, or the very early years of the new century, the story becomes much less of Jennie Dean herself and more of her major accomplishments, the founding and establishment of the Manassas Industrial School. As recited previously, it would seem that it was hers to conceive, to plan for, to establish and set going with a host of preceptors, advocates, workers, donors and interested notables from the world of philanthropy and education, all of whom she had been able to win as Mr. Villard has so aptly stated in a recent letter to me, without a remarkable personality but rather through a sheer simplicity in approach and an uncringing but straightforward mannerism which won her friends and "believers" wherever she went. She built the foundation for another miniature Hampton or Tuskegee, the institution phase of which, and whose future success or failure, must now be passed to other hands than hers to minister, plan and perpetuate. I personally know that Jennie Dean never relinquished the moral responsibility for the success or failure of the institution even though she was to take but little or no part in its management or program of action in years ahead. It was her project, born of her fertile and sympathetic mind and a part of her very life and being. She could perhaps, place the responsibility for every act of omission or commission in the years that ensued, upon shoulders other than hers, but "down deep in her very soul" she unquestionably felt that the moral responsibility was still hers.

Miss Dean had interviewed, sought and interested many outstanding folk then in public life and had personally persuaded persons from this outstanding group to take official and responsible positions in the management and planning of the school. That some of these persuaded folk had been the means of either creating dissension or had been the focus about which much dissension radiated, undoubtedly created within Miss Dean's mind the thought that the mistake was basically hers–if mistake it was. It may even be that she many times during these years regretted that she had invited some of those outstanding personalities into the picture because of the part that their entering it had upon her future relationship to "Her Work." To say the least, the situation became more and more complicated insofar as her part in it was concerned and Jennie Dean, the real Jennie Dean, seems to have been interred long before she died insofar as her active influence in her project was concerned.

XII

The School Chartered, Began Its Work in 1894

ON a slip attached to data furnished by the principal of the school, Rev. W.H. Barnes, appears these questions: "Did you know that Miss Jennie Dean began to get funds or set to raise funds for the proposed school in 1891? Associated with her was a southern white woman, a Virginian, Miss Jane E. Thompson? That Dr. Edward Everett Hale in April 1891 issued a circular from his office asking friends in Boston to contribute?" These and other questions might be easily asked of the biographer and are questions answered only by records to which he has not had access and constitute a part of the uncompiled data which makes the use of specific dates during these early years of Miss Dean's work a questionable procedure. But these items help to sustain the suggestion that Miss Dean had actually begun work on her institutional project long before many of the characters hereinafter named had entered the picture. The name of Miss Jane E. Thompson cannot be disassociated from that of Jennie Dean from the earliest date of her conceiving the idea and her plan for such an institution until her passing. Voluminous letter files perused, show that Miss Thompson remained loyal to Miss Dean until the last.

The Manassas Industrial School was chartered under the laws of the Commonwealth of Virginia October 7, 1893. The charter was drafted by the Hon. George C. Round of Manassas who acted as Chairman of the local committee. The original buildings and grounds were dedicated on Labor Day, September 3, 1894 with appropriate ceremonies. Prof. H.P. Montgomery of Washington, D.C., is recorded as its first president and Mr. John Clifford is listed as its first principal. He, however, proved to be only principal-elect, for it seems that Dr. Elijah P. Clemens actually served as the first principal though entering the activities of the school after the dedicatory exercises from which both he and Mr. Clifford were absent.

Miss Dean had reached the peak of her career insofar as actual personal accomplishments were concerned for these dedicatory exercises held on the grounds of the now established institution, were unquestionably largely of her own arrangement and we may well imagine her pride and gratitude in thus presenting to her public the host of newly made friends from both the South and North and her local supporters of both racial groups. The actual realization of a dream which she had made come true.

Notable in the long list of participants in the dedication on this remarkable September day, were such outstanding local folk as the Hon. E.E. Meredith, member of the House of Representatives from the Manassas District; Dr. H.M. Clarkson, Supt. of Prince William County Schools, a very distinguished son of the South and a southern gentleman of the old school, highly sympathetic towards the Negro group; The Hon. Chas. E. Nichol, Circuit Judge; William E. Lipscomb, County Judge; Hon. Geo. C. Round, Chairman of local committee, and who contributed much towards the dedication exercises, and a host of other local lights too numerous to mention.

Miss Jane E. Thompson of Fauquier County, faithful supporter of Miss Dean as has been outlined before, as much interested in the establishment of the school as Miss Dean herself, it would seem, donated the flag for the occasion which was presented by Capt. R.H. Tyler and received by the Rev. Marshall D. Williams of Manassas. This flag was "raised" by Miss Dean herself midst the acclaim of the assembled populace.

The dedicatory address was delivered by the Hon. Frederick Douglass whom the biographer saw for the first time and whose fine head, impressive figure and stentorian voice left an impression which time cannot erase. To present to the people of her section such a racial character as Frederick Douglass as an example of Negro possibilities in the face of the great handicap of slavery, was as much of an accomplishment from one angle, as the dedication of the school itself.

I deem it not an unnecessary waste of space to give some of the names of invited guests who either attended or sent messages of congratulations and well wishes. These names suggest the widest acquaintanceship and contacts in the interest of the School Miss Dean had made thus early in history. Among the long list were the names of Hoke Smith, of the Department of the Interior; William T. Harris, Commissioner of Education; John E. Massey, Supt. of Public Instruction, Gen. Eppa Hunton, U.S. Senator; Dr. J.L.M. Curry, Agent of the Peabody and Slater Funds; Dr. Wm. W. Smith, President of Randolph Macon College, Edward Everett Hale of Boston, William A. Slater of Conn., Miss Clara Barton of Red Cross fame, Miss Emily Howland who donated the first building, Mrs. Ellen S. Mussey of Washington, D.C., who became a staunch supporter of the school also, and many others of national standing.

Associated with the School at this time and for some years later, were such outstanding white local characters as Mr. Round, already mentioned, Mrs. E.B. Dodge, Mr. Abraham Conner, Mr. J.B.T. Thornton, all of whom served in some official capacity in connection with the School or gave encouragement to the movement for thus bettering Negro life.

I think it safe to say that this one BIG DAY for Miss Dean must have meant the apex of happiness in her life. I can conceive of no other occasion in her life when public acclaim and appreciation for her efforts reached such proportions. With all that followed, the biographer is proud to be able to record and emphasize this big moment of happiness which must have been hers. The memory of this occasion might have been the healing balm which stayed the pain during the sadder years of her closing life.

In October 1894 the School was opened and began its first session in the dwelling house formerly used as a residence by the former owner, Howland Hall, the gift of Miss Emily Howland of New York, not yet being completed. Six students constituted the actual first enrollment but soon increased to seventy-five according to Miss Dean's own statement in her auto-biographical sketch before recited.

Dr. E.P. Clemens was then in charge of the School as principal. The details of these years have a direct personal appeal for I was then a student–during the infancy of the school, entering there in 1898 and graduating with the third class in 1900. I was there during the first fire and have a very vivid memory of the transfer of the classes to the old unfinished church building, so well described by Miss Dean in her quoted sketch in previous chapters. These were trying days for Jennie Dean and proved her own personal mettle and growing influence she had with many outstanding folk who had aided her previously and came to her rescue again and again.

I am reminded here of a recent letter from Mr. Villard, who, in commenting on my original copy of this story, had this to suggest: "I think that you could tell a little bit more about Jennie Dean's own looks and personality and how it was that she won all those white friends and counsellors of the North. That was really a remarkable achievement, because she was not an orator; she had not the charm and personality of Mrs. Bethune. I think it was her own straightforward honesty and refusal to pretend to be anything else than what she was, a plain woman, unashamed of being a cook who made money to help the School and her people. I was much interested by the deep impression she made upon my Southern wife. There was nothing servile about her; she did not play up to or toady to the whites. She was just a plain, simple, dignified black woman with no gift of oratory and no charm beyond what I have said–her straightforwardness and sincerity."

In this one paragraph from his letter, Mr. Villard has saved me many words and pages for in addition to this achievement and capacity, it is even a greater tribute to her to state that to win the Southern home friends to her cause first as a basis upon which to start the movement for the School, she overcame much greater handicaps of prejudice, disregard for Negroid capacity for schooling and training, intolerance and indifference as to the Negro's possibilities as a citizen of the local regions, State and Nation, than she had to overcome in winning more liberal minded friends of the North and East.

XIII
The Little Oak Begins Its Fight for Maturity

INVESTIGATION of the original charter, copy of which has been loaned by the present principal, Rev. W.H. Barnes, proves a contention raised by Miss Jane E. Thompson, Miss Dean's most loyal early Southern supporter, in some of her correspondence made available to me–that the name of Miss Dean did not appear on this basic legal document. Why? There are many reasons advanced by those I have interviewed and perhaps we can dismiss this seeming unfortunate oversight, if oversight it was and the reasons therefore, as an item interred with the body of Jennie Dean.

The document shows the following incorporators: Rush H. Shippen, President; Henry P. Montgomery, Jane E. Thompson, Emma V. Montgomery, Henry F. Baker, James H. Merriwether, Lucy S. Doolittle, James H. Bradford, Marshall D. Williams, Henry H. Waring and George C. Round, so recorded in the Clerk's office of Prince William County as of October 10, 1893.

Just how long Mr. Shippen remained president is not on record but the name of H.P. Montgomery soon appears in the records as president. Just prior to the dawn of the new century, possibly about 1898, Carroll D. Wright, then Commissioner of Labor in the Federal Government, became the first established president and seems to have remained in charge of the School's administration until 1905 when the character about whom much has already been told and who figured in its administration and history for more than two decades–Oswald Garrison Villard–became the predominant figure about whom surged many elements of progress in the school's growth and development but also many raging torrents of discontent due to his program and policies and the failure of many proposed plans of action.

The reign of Mr. Wright it seems, catered more to sentiment than to direct business procedures and upon the accession of Mr. Villard as Chairman of the Board and President, an attempt was made to put the institution upon a business basis. Mr. Villard brought to the School a background of abolition history as the grandson of William Lloyd Garrison coupled with what was then considered a keen business mind as owner and publisher of one of the Nation's leading journals, the *New York Evening Post*. He was wealthy in his own right; influential in national circles and had in a degree, continued his grandfather's interest in the welfare and progress of the colored people. Through Miss Dean's influence with outstanding folk in Washington and New York, Mr. Villard became her personal choice, upon the recommendation of these influential supporters.

In the meantime, Dr. Clemens who came as the first principal, had fallen into disfavor with the Wright administration and had been replaced with E.H. Woodford a product of Berea College, Kentucky. A fine gentleman, a fine scholar and a sympathetic administrator, beloved by all the students (I was a graduate under him). Though many improvements came under his leadership, he too soon incurred disfavor of the ruling powers, and after two or three years, became the victim of a growing inside conspiracy which was to eventually wreck many promising careers of those induced to either become principals or join the faculty.

It is very difficult to go into an accurate chronology of the succeeding principals and faculty members because of the lack of reliable existing records and if inaccuracies occur in the recital, it is due to this fact. The same element is involved in listing the various administrative regimes for so many changes in principals occurred during the life of the institution as a private school, that records of past principalships were given but scant attention by the successors and most of those existing were either destroyed or scattered. This one element has made very hard and te-

The Little Oak Begins Its Fight

dious the biographer's attempt at chronological order in this narrative.

Mr. Villard became the president of the Board in 1905. The school had continued to grow and aside from the re-erection of buildings destroyed by fire, shop buildings had been added and the farm much improved and put on a somewhat healthy productive basis. The student body had increased to near the 150 mark and the faculty had been considerably increased. Donations continued to come in through Miss Dean's field efforts and many new friends had been won to the cause, among whom were Mrs. Ellen Mussey and a corps of other equally prominent figures in the educational and philanthropic world. Mr. E.H. Woodford had been succeeded by Prof. William C. Taylor, also of Berea College, Kentucky as the third principal and under his scholastic leadership, the curriculum was much advanced and the faculty much improved. Agriculture became a pre-eminent part of the vocational phase of the school's educational program and with the special training of Prof. Taylor in this field, the dairy was developed and stock raising both for student consumption and revenue purposes, became a very productive source as well as fine training for both boys and girls. Gardening on a large scale was developed and the trades department to high efficiency.

During these years Miss Dean had served for a while as matron and general supervisor of the girls and of the domestic side of the institution. Her position in the inner circles of management and policy shaping, had gradually been reduced to the minimum and aside from the field work in securing donations for the School, she was virtually relegated to the role of a mere looker-on. What had been her child, born of her own mind and body, and whom she had nurtured through the difficult period of infancy; sacrificed for, labored for and prayed for; had now been taken from her and seemingly taught to ignore her. Figuratively, the little oak she had planted, maternally nurtured and cared for in the early years of its growth, watched its growing roots take firm hold in the soil about it and witnessed its growth to that of a rapidly maturing tree, was to have her tender care and watchfulness no longer. It was not hers to warn against cutting a branch here or scarring the trunk there or to see that the soil was kept fertile and well banked about its base as a safeguard against storms ahead. She, it seems, could only wishfully admire her child of the soil at a distance and hope that some day again, it might be within her realm of duty to minister to it.

XIV

Some of the Early Characters

IT might be fitting here to pay tribute to some of the early characters who were on the roster of the first faculty, some of whom are still living and have given the biographer much help in opening their files for inspection and in personal interviews which have proven invaluable. Among those living is Miss Mary E. Vernon, now Mrs. Mary Vernon Ware the first woman member of the original faculty who came to the School when it first opened as cooking teacher, matron and literary teacher. Mrs. Ware now living in retirement in Washington, D.C., gave yeoman service to the School in these pioneer days and it was she who firmly established what is now the splendid modern domestic science department of the now Regional High School but still by the official name, the Manassas Industrial School. Mrs. Ware left the institution in or about 1904 and became connected with the domestic science department of the school system of Washington, D.C., and it is from long years of service in this system that she is now retired.

Miss Bessie Loving, now Mrs. Bessie Loving White and residing in Manassas as principal of the Brown School there, was another of the pioneer faculty members, coming to the school in 1897 as matron, sewing teacher and literary teacher as well. Mrs. White gave most loyal service to the institution for more than ten years and retired to enter the public school system of Prince William County with which she is still engaged. She became the wife of Mr. John W. White during her connection with the School, who will also be mentioned as among the pioneers. Both reside in Manassas.

Mr. John W. White came to the School in 1897 as assistant principal and also served as literary teacher, commandant of the boys' cadet corps which he established and served in this capacity until about 1904. He then left the School and entered the Government service in Washington, D.C. In 1907, he was recalled as Business Manager and in 1908 became Business Manager and Treasurer. Following this two year service he re-entered the Government service from which he retired in 1941. Many were the sacrifices made by this pioneer group of faculty members who served the first year without pay. There were others but I mention only those now living. Only now, in late years, is there full appreciation for the service they rendered for each and all of them it seems became the victims of factional inside dissension and were let out with but little or no praise and with utter disregard for their future which had been painted so glowing to them when they were entreated to come to Manassas.

Under Mr. White's management the School financial system was revised and put on a modern basis. The principal's cottage was erected under his direction, stones for which foundation he hauled with the farm team. Much might be related in connection with his fine influence upon the boys of the School and community during his early years there and of his devoted attachment to the institution and its objectives. But in the ultimate from somewhere came the command "He must go," a command which grew into sort of a slogan as the years passed and many careers were accordingly wrecked thereby. If there are any individuals or group of individuals associated with the School's beginning and establishment who deserves honor and praise bordering on that deserved by Miss Dean herself, it is this pioneer group. All were summarily dismissed with the "unworthy" label attached and all soon established themselves in other fields of service where they have given a lifetime of appreciative and recognized service. The tenure of this group mentioned, represents the spirit of dedicated service of many other pioneers, and those who came later and rendered kindred service and received kindred treatment. Perhaps it was a nightmare of vagaries incidental to a growing child, deprived of its mother's tender care and becoming an experiment in the hands of many varying personalities.

XV

The Waning Influence of Miss Dean

WITH the coming of Mr. Villard as president and chairman of the Board, high promise prevailed that his influence would rally many new friends to the school. His agenda seems to have included weeding out much of the old material and the adoption of new plans of procedure. Vibrant in virile manhood, rich in experience, highly intelligent, well educated and keen in literary and business experience, Mr. Villard seems to have made the fatal mistake of correcting evils which he considered existed, overnight as it were. He, as it was mine to call to his attention many years later, overlooked the basic, traditional background which still enslaved the minds of the masses of colored folk whom he felt should rally at once, under his leadership.

It would appear that Mr. Villard failed to understand that insofar as the colored folk of the Northern Virginia area were concerned, these folk still looked upon the School primarily as a Jennie Dean project. As crude as some of her plans and ideas may have seemed to him and his advisors at this stage of the institution's progress, these folk still looked to Miss Jennie Dean as the basic moral force back of it all and for at least a participating leadership. When the beacon of her influence shone bright, their interest was enhanced and keen. When it dimmed, their interest waned proportionately. As a comparison, imagine what would have happened to Tuskegee in the corresponding stage of its development without the dynamic force of Booker T. Washington and his vision and influence back of it.

It would seem, viewing the situation in retrospect that the adoption of a program of gradual change along with the cultivation of an understanding of the need of this change as a medium of holding the interest of the masses, would have produced results he desired and would have, it is felt prevented much of the discord and dissension which took on form and action. The financial condition of the institution was improved but the general public morale was lowered by these arising factional tirades. Miss Dean who had been ever at the forefront as the focus of all planning for the School's future, was soon relegated to the sidelines and designing and over-ambitious personalities came to the forefront as the administration's local spokesman. Mistrust of each other's motives took firm hold of many of those in the inner councils and reporting trivial incidents of faculty and domestic life at the School to the "Big Boss" from whom came too often, summary action, made life miserable for many of those whose loyalty might have been unquestioned. Many were the principals and teachers and officials summarily dismissed and for years each school term began with a minority of the original faculty re-employed. After three years on the Board, I resigned because of this reason. It is not for me to say that all of these dismissals necessitating changes in faculty and official personnel were not without merit, but it seems as a whole to have been a rather ruthless method of proposed constructive progress. The future records of most of those dismissed, proved beyond question that they might have been retained to the great advantage of the institution.

Miss Dean, herself, became a victim of this ruthlessness for it seems decreed and substantiated by records of Miss Thompson who remained loyal to Jennie Dean until her death, that she was definitely out of the picture even as a counsellor. Miss Thompson wrote of the May 30, 1908 Board meeting, "You remember what was said at the May 30th. meeting (1908) 'Jennie Dean can no longer represent this Board for she misrepresents us.' " This is a mere sidelight on the waning influence of Miss Dean and the depths to which she had fallen within a little more than a decade after she had founded the School. The story of the effect of

The Waning Influence of Miss Dean

this treatment and how it unquestionably contributed to her early demise, will be related later.

With Miss Dean relegated to the scrap heap, there arose a new local leadership which held the reins for some years, worked hard to build where others had failed, but which was sadly lacking in those sterling qualities of leadership which were inborn in her. Her counsel was not needed by those in power and it is unquestionably true that her untutored mind could not comprehend the more modern trends in education and business procedures. But to ignore her capacity for genuine common sense, to throttle her desire for a word of counsel in the management of the thing she had created, to literally tear from her breast her nursing child and cast it to those with a questioned sympathy towards it, seemed as cruel as it proved to be unwise.

XVI
An Era of Trial and Balance

THE story of the School brings us now to about the year of 1907. The strain of the preceding years began to take its toll upon the health of Jennie Dean. She appeared no longer the vibrant energetic disciple for the cause, capable of prolonged periods in the field in search of friends and funds for the institution. Advancing years, added to her apparent disregard for her bodily welfare when personal sacrifice was a definite part of her daily routine, began to undermine her strength. Mental confusion had evidently begun to overcome her former calm selfconfidence. Bitterness at her plight as a mere sideline observer whose counsel was only occasionally sought and then it seems, patronizingly only; unquestionably contributed much to the beginning of her physical decline and she was now spending much of her time in the solitude of her Catharpin home.

As Dr. Leslie Pinckney Hill recites in a recent communication to me, "When I came to Manassas in 1907, Jennie Dean had done her pioneer work. Ill health was to be her unhappy portion throughout the time I personally knew her. Her visits to the School were now and then and her personal appearances were fewer and fewer. There was never a moment, however, when she was not profoundly interested in everything that happened at Manassas and in everybody who had a hand in it. She had a vision of a school that would give a practical breadwinning education to Negro youth, and would bring together the Southern white man and his Negro neighbor, along with such philanthropists from the North, as might help with the development of the institution, without undue interference with local autonomy. This vision was never dimmed. She brought to the realization of it a homely, native philosophy and mother wit, and a very intense sincerity and enthusiasm with which she could carry any audience, North or South."

The history of the institution up to this point had been much akin to that of the growth and development of an individual youth from infancy to childhood and on into adolescence–with all of the vagaries incidental thereto. Experimentation was most natural and due to the increasing changes in local administration and faculty, seems to have been carried to the extreme in all too many instances. Principals came and went and with them too often, many of the faculty. This placed the institution at a very serious disadvantage for it deprived the school of a permanent, satisfied, interested group of administrators and teachers and departmental heads who could map out a program or curriculum with a degree of hope that they might follow it through, make corrections and alterations where necessary and adjust their private lives to the services required of them and their sacrifices and yet plan for a future with the institution.

But an already established tradition even this early, left each newly employed principal and teacher doubtful as to the tenure of his connection with the School and surely this condition did not contribute to his giving his best service nor did it contribute to the general faculty and administrative morale, however devout each individual may have been in his service and loyalty. Wm. C. Taylor whose services have been referred to previously, as principal succeeding E.H. Woodford, ultimately gave way to George Mays. The term of Mr. May's service bespoke a degree of progress and some innovations in curriculum and of course many changes in the faculty. Discordant elements soon arose, however, and he was succeeded in 1907 by Leslie Pinckney Hill who came to the institution following service on the faculty of Tuskegee. Mr. Hill, a Harvard graduate, seems to have had the full endorsement of Mr. Villard who had assumed the chairmanship of the Board in 1905. He brought to the School, scholarship, experience in similar work at Tuskegee, virile youth and a potent vision. With the full backing of Mr. Villard, he was given a somewhat free rein to correct some of the evils in administration which had so perplexed the school management previously. That he tackled the job with both vim and determination is evidenced in the many changes which occurred during his six year term. In fairness to him, I shall let him speak for himself. In a recent letter from him citing his experience briefly, he said, "For six years I gave to the work at Manassas unstinted and unremitting labor. Although I found there a very complicated institutional and community roster of problems and a widespread skepticism, because of a long series of administrative difficulties and failures. I found also that it was possible to slowly gather about the work a group of unselfish, local friends, among whom I always counted you, whose unprejudiced interest was in the development of the School for the Negro population of Northern Virginia. Then, in close cooperation with Mr. Oswald Garrison Villard, Chairman at that time of our Board of Trustees, I was able in New York, Boston, Cleveland and Chicago, to build up Manassas clubs or associations of liberal white friends with whom I kept in steady, personal contact, and through whom we gained in time, a broadly extended interest in our program resulting after a while, in a gratifying measure of financial support. This work abroad was very exacting in time, energy and thought, but it was practically very fruitful. So urgent was the need in those days, and so important the people who developed confidence in us, that I did not know what it was to get tired. The job was thought impossible, but it was done."

"When I arrived at Manassas there was no home for the principal and his family. I had to go out personally and raise money for this fundamental need. Our dormitory facilities were distressingly inadequate. We had no proper housing either for classroom instruction or the prosecution of our trades. There was an old barn improperly placed for adequate uses on the farm. Physically, the School presented a sobering challenge. It was my good fortune to purchase by sweat and anxiety untold, some relief from these distressing conditions." Mr. Hill further relates how instruction was improved through the building of a revised curriculum and in bringing the institution up to a point of recognition by its program of secondary education and its departments of trades and agriculture. He tells of the State recognition of the Summer School for teachers and of its support by the State of Virginia; of its farmer's conference, stimulating community interest and of an established program for better homes, better farms, better schools and of building for community and regional confidence and finally of definitely working towards a better understanding of mutual problems by the whites of the community and region and a more direct cooperation on the part of the two racial groups.

This, it would seem, was progress as Jennie Dean herself would have desired it and planned it in her own way even though she may not have been capable of conceiving its more modern trend. But as Mr. Hill has stated, her failing health and other conditions, left her at this time almost completely out of the picture. Her most ardent sympathizers felt that she was purposely ignored and that "The Work" was being taken wholly out of her hands; out of control of the host of friends she had made and out of the hands of the Negroes of Northern Virginia. Factionalism became rife for a time and the Rev. D.G. Henderson, Miss Dean's Catharpin pastor and one of the most ardent workers for the establishment of the School, and a trustee, offered a resolution of protest before the Baptist Association of Northern Virginia, charging that there was a definite program in the making by the general management of the institution, to replace all Negroes on the Board of Trustees by Northern Whites. In this movement of protest, he had the backing and support of Miss Jennie E. Thompson, a southern white woman who had fought and sacrificed with Miss Dean in behalf of the establishment of the School and who had demonstrated her loyalty and lack of prejudice racially, throughout the preceding years of her activity. With the removal of this cloud, others appeared.

Thus the regime of Mr. Hill, while markedly progressive from one angle, was not without its turmoil and obstacles to transcend. During this period the gift of Mr. Carnegie of the administration and trades building said to have cost more than $30,000, was an outstanding accomplishment and whether through the influence of Mr. Villard and Mr. Hill or a combination in which Miss Dean herself figured–for though she was virtually inactive, her influence

An Era of Trial and Balance

was still potent as Mr. Carnegie himself acknowledged in one of his later annual gifts to the School. This was the largest single contribution and perhaps the most outstanding the School had received because it came at a point in the institution's history when it did the most good in boosting the public morale and interest in the School's growth. It attached the name of America's foremost philanthropist and the world's then outstanding industrialist to the Jennie Dean roster of friends she had personally won for "The Work." It is of particular interest to note that Mr. Carnegie prior to his gift of the administration or library building which was dedicated in 1910 had been an annual contributor to the School.

Mr. Villard in his reference to the School in his autobiography "Fighting Years," had this to say on the subject of Mr. Carnegie. "Here I must gratefully acknowledge most generous help from Andrew Carnegie who first came to our aid with a check for $1,000.00 without solicitation because of an article of mine. I flattered myself that it was my moving picture of the School's needs which had brought this check. Not at all; he told me he sent it because the name of Jennie Dean reminded him so of the Scott's heroine of the Midlothian, Jeannie Deans! Later, Mr. Carnegie gave us a library building but with the warning that no library should ever go beyond 100,000 books. When I asked him what one did when one passed the 100,000 mark? He said 'Give away the oldest.' In the depression of 1907, I tremblingly asked him for a renewal of his $1000.00. He said 'In these times? Absolutely not! I'll give you $2000.00.' His check for that sum was annually forthcoming until he died."

While the School during these years received many large gifts and much improvement in grounds, buildings and curriculum was evident, the cost of operating became correspondingly increased and the nightmare of increasing debt began to develop. It is meant that an ever-increasing income from donors must be produced as the income from the small endowment would not suffice to offset the annual deficit. The income from operation was akin to that of all similar private educational institutions; way below the cost of operating costs. As old contributors died or slackened in their support, new ones must be found. Jennie Dean was out of action and the influence from her former field activities was being seriously felt. When she had formerly lost one friend, she had invariably found a new one. Her "Child" had found nourishment often when she had to be denied it. There was no longer a Jennie Dean to approach the threshold of the old donors or that of prospects she knew how to find and approach, and win. The School had unquestionably reached its zenith of growth and development as a private institution for the thralldom of increasing debt had enmeshed it.

The approaching World War was to further complicate the economic picture, with alteration of the whole national financial structure, the changes in tax standards hitting wealth and corresponding philanthropy hardest. Community chests grew out of former private charity. Foundations superceded private gifts to education and other kindred institutions. Charity and philanthropy took on a definite scientific phase and was now to to be distributed through organized agencies devoted to that alone. All this was unforeseen at this stage of the School's existence, but with this unsurmountable economic obstacle just a few years ahead, it was all but impossible to escape from a hopeless financial situation.

XVII
"Not Dead But – Sleepeth"

AS the twilight ebbed to darkness on May 3rd 1913, the soul of Jennie Dean took final leave of its mortal casement. Perhaps the minister at the funeral announced her earthly tasks finished. If this were true, the story I am writing would surely end here. All of her life's efforts had been directed towards a main obejctive; that of building for better, more productive and progressing living among her people. The establishment of missions, chapels and churches, community missionary and social service work were all preliminary steps preparatory to that main objective; a progressive objective with a fully completed program of action and living, and educational institution for the influencing of human minds and lives. The establishment of this institution was but a single stage in a program she had conceived and started in operation. As long as it operates for the chief purpose for which it was established, however, varying in its program, it will remain an incomplete task of Jennie Dean in which her living influence will continue to figure.

Her mortal remains are interred in the churchyard cemetery of a church she founded as a mission and saw grow to full maturity. Obscure and somewhat neglected is the place of burial but bright and gleaming, with an increasing brilliance as the years pass, is the influence of a life lived for others in unselfish and constructive service to humankind. Such a task as hers will remain progressively unfinished as long as there is need for the type of service she sought to render.

In connection with the Commencement Week exercises May 25, 1913, a memorial service for Miss Dean was arranged by principal Hill. The writer was the Alumni speaker on this occasion and like even the memorial speakers, Kelley Miller, Leslie Pinckney Hill, the principal and Gordon Battle, he was wholly unequal to the task as he now sees it. Because of the inactivity of Miss Dean during the years of her illness, the public spotlight had been removed from her and thrown to others. There was not accordingly a real and full appreciation of what she accomplished and of her real worth as a public benefactor. It has taken the years since to develop this full appreciation. I am putting to words now the best I know how, the eulogy I wish I might have been able to deliver on that occasion. It is my hope that in the writing of her life story and its ultimate publication and distribution throughout Northern Virginia at least, that there may be created an interest in the movement to remove her mortal remains to the campus of the School 'neath a fitting and dignified memorial shaft. Where stands the present memorial bronze plaque where once stood Charter Cottage, the original farm house, and which memorial I was instrumental in placing there, might be the proper site.

The title of this chapter dedicated to the passing of Jennie Dean as a physical being–"Not Dead But Sleepeth," was taken from the grave monument which bears in addition "In Memory of Jennie Dean, 1852 - 1913, Founder of the Manassas Industrial School." To those who pause at the last resting place of Jennie Dean, in the little, lonely church cemetery at Catharpin, these latter gravestone words speak volumes. Thus the physical Jennie Dean retires behind the curtain of eternity with "The Work" to be carried on by other minds and hands. She left a heritage in which her spirit will continue vital as long as the institution she founded exists and in whatever form of action, but so long as it continues to contribute to the advancement of the youth of Northern Virginia. The story continues now as mostly the story of the School.

XVIII

The Attempt for State Aid or Control

MR. HILL after six years as principal, finally accepted a position at Cheney Institute, Cheney, Pennsylvania, now a Pennsylvania State Teacher's College. As Dr. Leslie Pinckney Hill, he is now the head of that institution and has been continuously, since leaving Manassas in 1913. According to incomplete records and from memories which are not infallible, including my own, he was succeeded by Mr. William J. Decatur whose administration was short in years (no record of how long) and of which there is no available record of the outstanding events of this administration.

If the order of succession is correct, he was followed in office as principal, by Mr. Fred D. Morton who remained about four years according to information given me, but of whose term of office and length of service there is likewise no official record available. Mr. Morton strove to build up the morale of the institution and to improve the literary curriculum, but like his immediate predecessors, was handicapped with the mounting indebtedness. He was successful only in part, in carrying out his program however meritorious it might have been and was not long in winning the disfavor of the upper bracket management and resigned. The year of his retirement is not of record but if, as I am told he was succeeded by Mr. Howe, it must have been in 1920.

One of the many improvement ventures started and completed between the years of 1905 and 1915, was the

Berwind Hospital, the gift of Mr. John E. Berwind. This building situated just behind the group of main buildings near the grove, was operated as a School Hospital and Clinic and it seems, was also meant to serve the community as well. Miss Eva P. Lewis (writer's sister) a trained nurse who was then practicing her profession in Prince William and the surrounding counties and the first trained nurse in the area, was put in charge of the hospital with Dr. Benjamin Iden as the physician in attendance. She carried on the work there for a number of years largely without pay. The hospital was ultimately abandoned in 1917 or thereabout, and became a guest house until ultimately completely abandoned from that use and became an employee's residence.

On January 8, 1920, Mr. Edward D. Howe, long a member of the Board of Trustees, a native of the area in which the School is located and who had been associated with Miss Dean in all of her missionary and religious activities since early youth, was elevated from the Board of Trustees to the principalship. He brought with him a background of experience rich in all the details of the School's operation from the beginning and intimate knowledge and acquaintanceship of and with the Negro and white folk of this Northern Virginia area. As both teacher and co-religious worker with Miss Dean in this area, it seems the Board desired to capitalize upon this experience and knowledge and for the first time, local leadership was entrusted to a native son.

I desire to state here in all fairness to principals about whose administrations only passing mention is given, as well as many other characters associated with the institution's history and fully worthy of detailed mention, that this passing mention is due largely to the absence of records of these administrations as well as the absence of information available to me of any outstanding events of these administrations which might add to the value of the story.

Now back to the Howe administration, of which there is much on record and during which many outstanding events occurred. During a large part of this administration, I was a member of the Board.

In a memorandum which included much data covering his incumbency as principal, Mr. Howe furnishes many details of the events leading up to his election as principal. Let him speak of some of these details: "I first met Miss Dean at Kettle Run School in a meeting agitating the needs of the School in 1892. I was then teaching in a public school at Brentsville, Va. Somehow, and I cannot now tell just why, I became interested in her project and through the years which followed, she would insist upon my going with her to the various meetings to speak in the interest of industrial education as a need for our girls and boys. Her "Northern Virginia" at that time was very limited but constituted more than a day's travel by horse and buggy, in many cases. I recall trips with her to upper Fauquier, lower Fairfax, all over Prince William and to Alexandria, etc. At these meetings we solicited anything we could get of help in the projected movement from doughnuts to dollars. Ultimately going on the Board, I became well acquainted with the growing problem of debt and the ever-changing administrations. The administration of Mr. Hill began with many changes in business procedure which bespoke, it seems to me, the application of 'big business methods to a poverty-stricken institution.' Expansion was begun on begged borrowings. The geographical area or sphere of influence was extended to the Blue Ridge Mountains on the west and to the Rappahannock on the south. An attempt was made to poll the interests of all the Negro people in this enlarged Northern Virginia area through organized agencies in every field of community endeavor. Years passed but debts lingered, reduced here but multiplying all too rapidly there. New executives followed in rapid order with [George] Mays, [William J.] Decatur, [George W.] Sampson, [Fred D.] Morton, and [Emma Lee] Williams and others taking the helm but accomplishing but little in stemming the tide of pressing debt. It was perhaps not realized then as much as later, just how much Jennie Dean's active service was needed in bringing to the School new friends and new donors. With chaos at the door, I was called from membership on the Board on which I had served eight years, to the principalship and installed January 8, 1920."

The administration of Mr. Howe was characterized by the enlargement of the geographical area of Northern Virginia in which the institution might find additional influence and corresponding support. His familiarity with the area and its folk and communities therein, much of which was virgin field insofar as contact in the direct interest of the School was concerned, took him over wide areas in his new campaign. He sought to curtail expenses, increase production on the farm and arouse continued interest on the part of old supporters, while ever seeking new ones.

Perhaps the outstanding activity of the Howe administration was the movement advocated by him and adopted as a possible economic panacea of last resort, was that seeking to have the state of Virginia by legislative enactment, either take over the institution as a State operated school or in appropriating bi-ennially towards its support. For two successive legislative terms, Mr. Howe canvassed the members of both houses of the Legislature over the entire State, seeking support for this movement, which it seems, had been endorsed by the Superintendent of Public Instruction and by the then governor. His slogan was "We the People, Save the State. Let the State Save the School." Public support was aroused in support of the plan for saving the School from closing because of the accumulated debt and the movement had the endorsement of much of the press locally and in adjacent territory. By narrow margin, the movement failed. In the General Assembly in 1923, the second legislative attempt, it was lost by only a few votes, having passed the House of the previous session but failing to reach a vote on the Senate calendar before final adjournment. Both bills carried a biennium appropriation of $10,000.00 towards the support of the School, according to Mr. Howe.

Thus it will be seen that the State control or even State ownership and operation was not a wholly new idea as many have thought when the more recent movement for County operation or ownership with State aid, was presented in or about 1933.

Mr. Howe succeeded in reducing the School debt from about $38,000.00 when he came in, to less than $24,000.00, when he was forced into retirement in 1924. Many were his personal sacrifices and likewise those of his faculty, to a large degree. But the same "inside" influence locally, which had wrecked the programs of so many other administrations, and with them the family fortunes, personal programs and careers, at least temporarily, got in its deadly work. Mr. Howe was "forced out" at the end of his school term in 1924, and the "parade of principals" continued. It was during most of his administration that I was then serving as a member of the Board and the continuation of this program of experimentation without a seeming warrant or purpose or constructive objective attained thereby, all convinced me personally, that both my time and energy were being wasted. In the face of our economic situation and general chaotic situation financially, a program in which malice and personal grudge played a more seeming important part than common sense and the application of basic business principles in dealing with petty problems of domestic administration, I resigned from the Board in 1924, feeling that the money expended in trips from my home in Harrisburg, Pa., could be more wisely and profitably spent in contributions to the general fund of the School. Thus I write more fully of Mr. Howe's regime because I personally know more of it.

XIX
The Parade Increases Its Tempo

IN seemingly rapid succession principal after principal followed during these troublesome years. Mr. Villard who had held the reins of executive authority since 1905 and who had done so much for the School during its era of progressive building or real growing stage, became less and less enthused with the support he was receiving, from the colored folk of the School's area of operation and influence. He felt that they were not doing their part in raising funds for the institution. On the basis of this charge of lack of interest on their part, he had threatened to resign from the Board on several previous occasions but in each instance, was prevailed upon to continue in office as Chairman of the Board of Trustees. Jennie Dean's influence and potential power of winning friends for the School and finding some Good Samaritan who might step in at the psychological moment with a contribution or donation to relieve the situation, had been lost. This influence of hers had been lost even many years before her death. Thus the whole economic and financial fabric was largely dependent upon the influence of Mr. Villard and his wealthy friends. His cooling enthusiasm for "The Work" had seemingly dampened the interest of his friends and other former donors, thus making the loss of Miss Dean's influence and activities even more tragic at this time.

The World War which was now passed, had as before referred to, changed the whole financial set-up governing private wealth. Income, inheritance and estate taxes, even involving gifts to private charity, had all but closed the doors to private charity as far as the School was concerned.

Foundations for such private fortunes, made very difficult the approach for financial aid. This fact had much to do with the campaign for the State aid under Mr. Howe. The School had reached its apex in constructive and progressive growth several years earlier, as I have already stated, now had reached its zenith in financial support and the trend began steadily downward.

Following Mr. Howe as principal, came Mrs. Emma Lee Williams for a brief period as acting-principal; followed by the recall of Prof. William C. Taylor, one of the earlier principals, who was persuaded to again take up the reins. He remained about two years and was followed by Mr. George W. Sampson for an equally short period and then by Mr. A.B. Edelin who in turn was followed by Mr. George Dudley.

In the meantime as of 1927, Mr. Villard after twenty-two years at the helm, resigned and retired from the leadership of the institution. He was succeeded by a member of the Board, Mr. T.C. Walker, a lawyer of Gloucester Court House, Va.

In connection with the ultimate passing from the active picture by Mr. Villard, I deem it wholly appropriate that I should recite an experience with him which bears so definitely upon his connection with and relationship to Manassas and the School. In 1939 Mr. Villard issued his book "Fighting years," an autobiography. In this splendid story of his life up to that time, his only reference to Manassas was a bit more than a page devoted to a recital of how he became acquainted with the School and Miss Dean's work and how he decided to identify himself with the institution. He tells briefly of his trials and tribulations and concludes the reference with this significant statement: "My work at Manassas was one of my outstanding failures but it gave me so clear an insight into the underlying problems, the weakness and shortcomings of the colored people that I have felt more than compensated for my time and trouble."

A copy of his life story was purchased by the present principal and it soon came to me that this reference to the School was an injustice to the institution and the cause it represented. I was permitted to read only this reference to Manassas from the book and soon an indignation meeting was held by the alumni group at the School, to which meeting I was summoned. It was decided to have the alumni make a reply to this assumed reflection upon the School. I was asked to draft that reply. However, I first insisted that I must have time to read the whole story of Mr. Villard and then I could correlate the reference to Manassas to the whole story. Upon completion of the reading, it was my personal decision that the reflection, if reflection it was, was more upon Mr. Villard than upon the School and cause. By common consent, I was permitted to draft a reply in which it was my basic hope to dissipate any bitterness which Mr. Villard entertained towards those with whom he had formerly worked and to prove to him that his work here had not been a "failure" in end-results. As he was in poor health at that time, as he wrote me, I wished to have him feel in these late years of his life, that there existed more appreciation for his services in this field of endeavor than he ever imagined and that the present generation held him in much higher esteem than when he passed from the picture of activity. My only fear, and that seemed the chief fear of Principal Barnes and the alumni group, was that this tort reference to "failure" in a book widely distributed, might result in alienating friends of the School which it badly needed and hoped to retain.

The concluding paragraph of my letter to him, for the alumni group read thus: "Frankly Mr. Villard, your labor at Manassas was not wasted effort however infinitesimal the end results may seem to you. To those of us who think they are capable of evaluating social and public service as a slow working process over a long period, your personal sacrifices and services here, loom large. We definitely feel that the implications on Manassas and on you as expressed in words 'outstanding failure,' constitute a weak link in the remarkable chain of events outlined in your splendid autobiography."

I quote his reply in full: "Dear Mr. Lewis, I am very much touched by your letter of December (1939) which I found on my return from Europe. I greatly appreciate the interest you have taken in my book and my statement therein in regard to Manassas and I am happy to have your assurance that my work for the School was not in vain, but it was a bitter disappointment to me for which I hold myself personally responsible in some degree, but not altogether. I left it in worse condition, except for the money put in then when I took hold. The failure of the colored people to cooperate adequately was a source of great discouragement to me in my work for the race.

"The concluding paragraph of your letter, I shall cherish always and sincerely hope that my words will not cause any discouragement among present friends of Manassas. It could have been a great school if the colored people had only had the loyalty and readiness to support the school which they should have had. At the end they promised definitely to raise the small sum I asked of them, to make it possible for me to continue with the work, but they failed and most of them were driving good automobiles at the time."

I offer no further comment on this incident and the correspondence involved and leave it with the reader as a part of the record and a sidelight on the story.

Mr. Walker, who had brought to the Board much experience in somewhat similar work in his own section of the State many years earlier, inherited a rather disorganized and seemingly discouraged organization with which to work. Many seemed to think that with practically an all-Negro management, there might result a rallying of the colored population in the area, to the School's support. Mr. Walker always full of fire and enthusiasm, tackled the job as best he knew how, but where he was able to rally one group, it seems he lost another's support. Factionalism soon became rife. Internal strife became rampant as the years went by and the debt continued to pile up. Every seeming remedy was tried but failed in most part. The debt scarecrow pauperized the energy of the workers for the School itself. It literally gnawed at the very vitals of the whole project from every seeming angle. There existed no dependable list of donors now for aside from the reasons above cited, Mrs. Hackley, Miss Howland, and many others, like Miss Dean, had passed from the earthly field of action and their influence with others as well as their personal donations, ceased with their passing.

Mr. Walker resigned as Chairman of the Board in 1933 and was succeeded by Dr. John D. Williams who had been placed on the Board as a direct successor to his father, Rev. Marshall D. Williams upon the occasion of the latter's death in 1925. Thus this family is the possible exception to the rule in that it has had continuous representation on the School's Board of Trustees since its founding. His father was one of the founders and remained on the Board until his passing.

Dr. Williams, our local physician and a graduate of the School, brought to the leadership a ripe experience with its problems. As a physician, he had endeared himself to the people of the immediate area in which the School was situated. He accepted the leadership with the definite understanding that it was to be only temporary and until they could find someone else. He remained Chairman until, and during the transition to the present three-county Regional High School and remains at present, Chairman of the original Board which holds the endowment fund and considerable acreage of the original farm tract. He is likewise an advisory member of the three-county Regional Board.

Carnegie Hall
The Administration Building

XX

Regime of Dudley Saw the School at Its Lowest Ebb

IN 1934 Mr. George Dudley, a graduate of Union University, became principal No. 13, if the records from which I have had to gather much of my data, are correct. He came at a time when the School debt, if not at its highest figure, was at a point of the most distressing proportions and the economic situation was seemingly hopeless. The student body had dwindled back to the lowest number since the early beginning of the institution, estimated by some, at below fifty. The physical plant had fallen into a state of tragic disrepair and there was no financial aid directly in sight. Thus Mr. Dudley, a veteran of the war, faced seemingly insurmountable obstacles. What Miss Dean might have done in a situation such as this, was a thought which perhaps did not enter the picture at all, for even the memory of her sacrifices and former accomplishments, gave way to a degree of panic superinduced by the increasing nightmare of bankruptcy and the total loss of the School property to its creditors.

Dr. Williams as the new Chairman of the Board put much of his personal funds into the project to stem the financial tide and keep the plant going. There was not even funds available for teachers' pay. Funds were drawn from the endowment fund and bonds were sacrificed. Only the loyalty of a small group of devout supporters of Dr. Williams' administration plus the continued rallying by the immediate community of Manassas and vicinity and the patience and sympathy of local creditors to whom little had been paid over many years, saved the situation. The School's standing with the white citizenship of Prince William County and the immediate Manassas community; its standing with the two local banks and the local business men among whom were most of its creditors, cushioned pressure of bankruptcy. The influence of Dr. Williams with these various elements above refered to, was another powerful factor in stemming the tide.

After about two years of arduous sacrifice, the health of Mr. Dudley began to show signs of succumbing to the effects of war service, not helped by the fact that neither he nor his teachers were receiving their full small salaries. Replacement of decadent equipment could not be made and as Dr. Williams puts it: "Dudley's last two years were years of depression bordering on famine and chaos." Little wonder that these years took their toll on Mr. Dudley's health and for this and other reasons, he retired in 1936.

During the last two years of Mr. Dudley's administration, a petition had been presented to the local county school board through its superintendent Mr. R.C. Haydon, by a delegation headed by Mr. Roscoe C. Lewis, a former teacher and former trustee and writer's brother–seeking county aid for high school students who wished to attend the School. As a result of this movement and Mr. Haydon's sympathy towards it, an arrangement was ultimately made by which Prince William County paid or contributed for at least one year or perhaps more, of which I am not sure–towards county students' tuition. This helped to increase the student attendance and perhaps to aid both morale and finances.

I think it wholly pertinent to observe here that it might have been the spirit of the Sainted Founder working through a Kind Providence which actuated both advocates for the School's continuance and its creditors who possessed the power and really had the moral right to close it. Just a few years ahead relief was pending and though those of us who had the vision of the possibility of its realization and had discussed among ourselves such an eventuality, yet none of us foresaw the regional high school plan as an immediate solution of the perplexing problem. I insist in my spiritual belief that the soul or spirit of Jennie Dean kept the fires of hope still burning in the hearts of those at the helm and bade them "Hold on, the Lord will Provide a Way Out," an expression which was common with her in her days of active trial and tribulation. Prayer and trust in her God was the main dependence of her life. It must have been that she inspired others to follow her example. There is not of record a single creditor who became seriously belligerent though many of them were seriously uneasy and had been patient over a long period of years. The School had been and still was, a community enterprise for good and it seems that these creditors locally, were more sympathetic than profit seeking in most instances.

XXI
The Parade of Principals Temporarily Ends

WITH the retirement of Mr. Dudley in 1936, following due negotiations and a brief survey on his part, Rev. William H. Barnes, serving at the time of his selection, as Director of Religious Education at Henderson Institute, Henderson, N.C., was chosen and installed as principal. The field was rife with opportunity for personal sacrifice and constructive service, a very dark general outlook, a much rundown plant and poor prospects for financial support. The one bright spot was the interest the County was persuaded to take in providing secondary education for the Negro children of Prince William County and during 1936 the arrangement for aiding such students within the county who matriculated with contributions for tuition aid as well as salary for an agricultural teacher, was continued.

During the first year of the principalship of Rev. Barnes, an approach was made to the County Supervisors of Prince William County seeking to interest them in taking over the School as a County High School. The Superintendent and Supervisors took the view that it was too big a job for one county to assume. Accordingly their interest was sufficient for them to seek the interest of two adjacent counties; Fairfax and Fauquier, which counties also had a small Negro population and a correspondingly small number of elementary graduates annually. The result of negotiations with these two counties mentioned, was enlisting their financial support in an experiment with the institution as a regional high and industrial school for one year.

During this year of experiment, feelers were put out by Superintendent Haydon to other adjacent counties and to the State Board of Education looking to cooperation and support in possibly making this experiment, if successful, permanent. In these approaches Mr. Haydon was joined by the authorities of Fairfax and Fauquier, through approaches to Dr. Sidney B. Hall, State Superintendent of Public Instruction and Dr. Fred M. Alexander, State Supervisor of Negro Schools.

In the meantime through the leadership of Dr. Williams, now executive head of the School, a public movement was started seeking public approval of a plan to sell the institution to the three-county regional setup for its bonded debt of approximately $16,000.00. In this movement, he had the support of most of the leaders among the Negro group of the geographical area concerned. A degree of success was attained in the administration of the School during this trial year in the face of many difficulties.

At the conclusion of the school year, the boards of the three counties cooperating in the year's experiment, agreed to purchase the institution and operate it as a Regional High School, subject to the approval of the School's own Board, based upon general public approval, through legal transfer. A series of public meetings were held putting the proposition before the Negro group in the various communities. Superintendent Haydon appeared before several of these group meetings, explaining the plan of action and the objectives sought. Finally on May 27, 1938 a public mass meeting held at the School itself, to which had been invited representation from every organized group interested in this institution, from all of the Northern Virginia area, and the Baptist Minister's Conference of Washington, D.C. At this meeting a resolution authorizing the transfer of the School and certain land areas, was drawn, discussed and finally adopted, under the supervision of the Board of Trustees. Under this resolution, the Board was authorized to proceed with the legal transfer of the property, preserving a certain number of acres of the farm land so as to make legal the existence of the original Board then in charge and to make secure and available the small endowment fund which it had been determined, could not be legally transferred. Another purpose of the continuation of the original board, was to perpetuate the original moral ownership of the institution and for public contact purposes.

The legal transfer and the recording of the deed soon followed. Thus the School was rescued from what for a time, seemed an untimely end and thus for the first time in its history there appeared reasonable assurance of its continued operation and maintenance.

It was thus readjusted to a new era of economics during which all such private institutions had to either change their plan of financing and operating, or close.

There were those who temporarily felt that Jennie Dean's dream and plan had been finally defeated. On the contrary, she had done for Negro education in this limited Northern Virginia area what Booker T. Washington had done for the Nation in the field of industrial education, many years before. She had sold the idea that Negro youth, like all other youth within the national group, could only be good and useful citizens when they were trained to be productive citizens with minds and hands coordinating in useful and productive work. Thus this change in the management, control and operation of the institution she had founded and established was but a necessary change in a program she had started, left to others to carry out and which like all other worthwhile and progressive movements, must conform to the changes in conditions in a changing world.

That these county officials welcomed the opportunity to make of it a regional high school at a price many times beneath its actual physical value, to say nothing of its worth as an educational adjunct to their present set-up, speaks volumes of praise to the Founder. That the State Department of Education, upon due investigation, was willing to finance the original setup and fully endorse the School's incorporation into the State educational system through a loan of $20,000.00 from its Literary Fund to a three-county board, constitutes another tribute to the wisdom and vision and constructive service Jennie Dean rendered both to the community and her State.

In a recent interview with Superintendent Haydon who

acts for the three-county board as chairman and director of the institution at present, he had this to say: "If Jennie Dean had not had the vision which was hers, the present situation could not have existed and the Negro youth might have been deprived of high school facilities for sometime to come. Her former work is thus recognized by the State Board of Education as a very definite and constructive movement. The School is considered by the State Department of Education as a pioneer in the regional high school movement." Thus with a guaranty of maintenance and support the School has a scholastic program with all departments standardized, including college preparatory, agriculture, home economics and building construction which includes carpentry, masonry, electricity, plumbing and steamfitting. In keeping with National Emergency, the School is at present offering Defense Courses in welding, electricity, cooking and agricultural mechanics. Standards for teachers have been raised with degrees and additional training required of all; teachers and officers regularly, if inadequately paid, the institution is now in a position to give even greater service than many of the recently established regional schools for secondary education, because of its long established institutional setup and its background of service and experience in the vocational field.

XXII

The School Today As a Regional High

THE School opened as a Regional High School of Northern Virginia with the term beginning 1938. The original name, Manassas Industrial School, was retained as the basic title, Northern Virginia Regional High being used as a sub-title. Its student roster immediately began to increase as bus transportation was provided to convey students from the counties of Fairfax and Fauquier. Approaches had been made by the Three-County Board, to other adjacent counties with small Negro student populations and Warren and Rappahannock counties soon became participating counties in the regional high plan, by providing their Negro elementary graduates with costs in the way of transportation allowances, being all inclusive. This year two or three other counties will cooperate.

Another accomplishment wrought in Prince William County was the providing of bus transportation for the elementary schools in connection with transportation of the high school students of the county. Consolidation of the Negro county schools was a necessary corollary to this transportation plan and thus again the establishment of the Regional High served relief and progress in two additional phases of improvement in the program of Negro local education. The writer advocated, drew and presented a petition to the County School Board three years before, urging these latter two improvements in the school program.

Thus, again, Jennie Dean enters the picture as the primary influence in these belated improvements in Negro county education in that but for her vision of such a school and its progressive influence, as Mr. Haydon has admitted, "these improvements might have been delayed for years." She might not have foreseen these direct accomplishments but there is little doubt but that she foresaw the ultimate breaking down of the inequality practiced with regard to Negro schools and the focusing of attention upon the need of providing adequate educational facilities for all.

When the present principal, Rev. W.H. Barnes, assumed charge of the school as a private institution in 1936, the student body had fallen well below the one hundred mark. Today its every facility is overtaxed and the enrollment at this writing, is well over the five hundred total. With a faculty of only five when he took charge in 1936, he now has under him, a faculty of seventeen with a complete general staff of twenty-two, five of this staff being special workers. Buildings have been renovated and a major improvement has been the installation of a modern sewerage disposal plant at an approximate cost of $22,000.00. A cottage has been provided and equipped modernly for home economics education. A program for general improvements of the grounds is under way and a movement definitely started looking to the erection at some future date, of the Jennie Dean Memorial Auditorium-Gymnasium.

The annual budget from public funds, has grown from about $1,500.00 at the beginning of the new project, to about $40,000.00 now, according to the present principal's statement. It may be thus easily seen that the heartaches and sacrifices endured by those who in these preceding years of seemingly inevitable disaster, were more than justified. I insist that there must have been some unseen power and force back of it all, which unquestionably inspired these valiants to hold on for a shift or calm in the tempest which might eventually present a definite break in the storm and a rift in the heavy hanging clouds which then overcast their skies. How fortunate that they did continue to hold on and to be present and actively on the scene when the renaissance did begin. Can it be said that Jennie Dean would have objected to this re-dedication of the institution she had founded, to the same objective in a different form?

XXIII

How Well She Builded And With What Success

THE story of Jennie S. Dean and her "UNDAUNTED FAITH" thus comes to a conclusion with the chief objective of her life of service and sacrifice attained and her seeming high purpose accomplished. It took her vision, sacrifices and original planning and her basic training in community social service and religious work, to give the one big movement she undertook, the vital spark of life and growth at the beginning. It required her mothering and winning of friends to the "cause" to give it an inspirational impetus and to fertilize its development. It took her influence to keep it alive when the dark days beset it.

Her philosophy of life was a philosophy of direct action based upon human needs; by both precept and example, leading and teaching in conformity with the creed of Jesus whose teachings she carried to youth and old age. She labored in the barren desert of humanity and produced flowering blossoms where nothing before had ever grown. By patient toil, she labored to erect a bulwark against idleness, ignorance, poverty and crime. She taught the dignity of labor and demonstrated how specialization in its various phases produced greater efficiency, more continuous and productive employment and thus lifted to a higher plane the morale of labor, however humble its role of action. She taught and proved that even a wilderness, dark and soggy and dreary, may become a paradise when God's undiluted sunlight is accorded a pathway of penetration into its entangling meshes. She showed to age and youth, how barren and rock-infested areas, abandoned to hopelessness and decay may become gardens of fruitful vegetation and plenty through coordination of the mind and the hand.

She taught that life is a privilege as well as a responsibility and that birth or origin have but little bearing on success or failure if the will to help one's self is cultivated and encouraged. She taught the life of Jesus Christ and lived it about as closely as any human could. She gave her ALL and asked only a reasonable response to her leadership and teachings, in return.

What she sacrificed for and accomplished in Northern Virginia, will remain a vital force for many generations to come whether in terms of Negro development or human development for Jennie Dean was more than a mere colored woman. She was a spiritually endowed power for good, transcending both race and creed, a woman of Faith and unafraid.

In her field of race relationship alone, her accomplishments are outstanding, for Jennie Dean's influence went far in teaching many southern whites in both private and public life, that an ignorant uneducated, untrained and idle Negro youth was a direct liability to both the community and State. That as a trained and respected citizen, with a definite assignment as part of human society, he could be and would be transformed into a valued asset.

That her influence carrying on as it did into the establishment of the School, an agency for building worthwhile citizenship and character and continuing now with a more generally accepted and modern program under county and State supervision–has much to do with the highly improved race relationship and cooperation as between the two citizenship groups of this area, is an acknowledged fact.

Her earthly tasks finished? No, no more than are those of the Christ she taught. She was a pioneer with a plan and a purpose. Her physical role was to set going a plan of human action too broad in scope for any one life to encompass its entire fulfillment. This plan of action was but a small item in the eternal and Divine plan of human progress and betterment. The good she accomplished will live even after the memory of it has faded and her name forgotten.

F-I-N-I-S

IN MEMORIUM

Stone marker and bronze plaque erected on Charter Cottage site in memory of the FOUNDER. Where stood the original farmhouse, now razed.

The photo above concluded Stephen Johnson Lewis' original *Undaunted Faith*. The historic photos and maps which follow have been compiled by The Manassas Museum for this Memorial Edition.

Jennie Dean had an abiding faith in Christian religion, and it was this, her friends say, that upheld her and helped her win success. Those who knew her intimately say she was cautious, prudent, self-sacrificing, with a personal character above reproach, and a spotless integrity . . .

Manassas *Democrat*, May 8, 1913

Photo: Newspaper photo of Jennie Dean
    Manassas *Democrat*, May 8, 1913
Source: Gift of Gloria Bennett-Jones

Photo Section

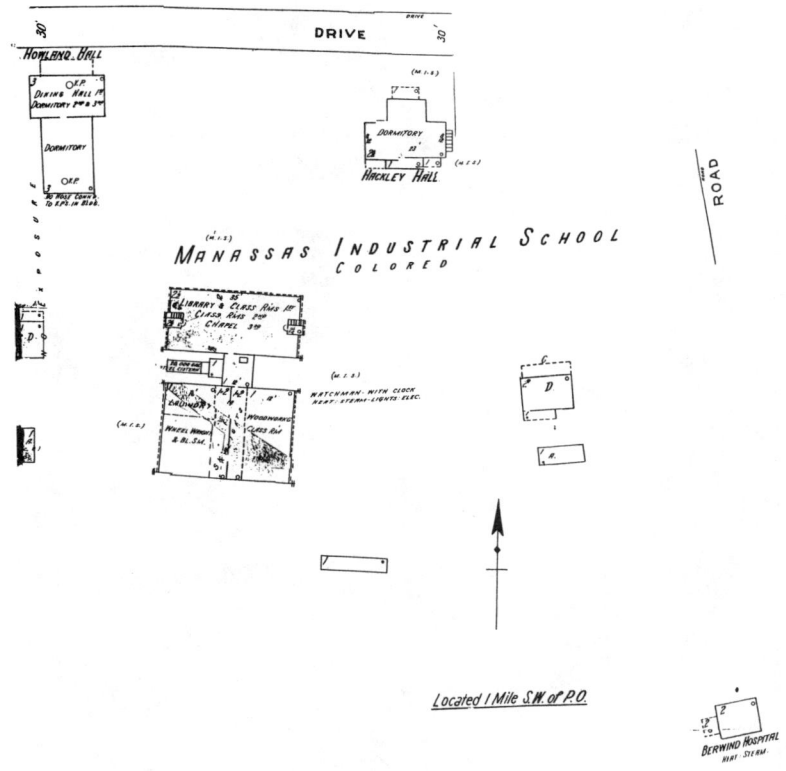

The school is desirably located, one mile from the town of Manassas, in Prince William County, Virginia. The school property consists of more than 200 acres of land ... and occupies a spot peculiarly appropriate, being near the battle ground of Bull Run.

1908-09 Catalog

Map: Sanborn Map Company, 1924
Source: Museum Collection

The course of study in this department extends over a period of three years. The students are taught the fundamental principles of the trade, from the cleaning of the shop, and the building of fires, to the shoeing of a horse, the repairing and building of a wagon, and the working of iron and wood in general.

1908-09 Catalog

Photo: Blacksmithing and Wheelwrighting, May 1911
Source: Gift of Jennie Dean Club

Photo Section

Agriculture, being the chief occupation of the Negro people, receives special attention at the school. The instruction is intensely practical, the text-book study being supplemented at every step by the daily care of the live stock, poultry, dairy, and by the productive cultivation of the 200-acre school farm.

1908-09 Catalog

Photo: Horse Barn, c. 1911
Source: Gift of Jennie Dean Club

Just as these colored boys and girls, half trained and therefore half discouraged, are leaving their unfinished grammar grade studies to take up miscellaneous jobs in the cities, Manassas takes hold of them and keeps them until they fairly master some trade by which they may earn an independent living, and at the same time be productive helpers of their communities.

1909 Financial Report

Photo: Cobbling and Shoemaking, May 1911
Source: Gift of Jennie Dean Club

Photo Section

We measure our progress in the degree in which we are daily saving Negro boys and girls from the dreadful clutches of ignorance, unthrift, poverty, and sin, and converting them by the most careful training and discipline into active, self-supporting men and women worthy of citizenship in the great republic.

1910 Financial Report

Photo: Senior Class, May 1911
Source: Gift of Jennie Dean Club

Photo: Berwind Hospital, May 1911
Source: Gift of Jennie Dean Club

The beautiful Berwind Hospital is the gift of Mr. John E. Berwind. It contains a boys' ward, a girls' ward, nurses' room, isolation rooms, kitchenette, sun porches, a hot-water heating plant and well-appointed bath rooms. The hospital has proved its value not only to the school but also the community, from which emergency cases are admitted upon the recommendation of the school physician.

1914-15 Catalog

Photo Section

Many of the men and women with their manual training were able to move into the world and become very successful citizens, able to handle their responsibilities and to contribute very much to the society in which they lived. Many followed through with professional training for the trades they acquired at Manassas.

Dr. William Waddell, DVM
Oral History Interview

Photo: Woodworking and Carpentry, May 1911
Source: Gift of Jennie Dean Club

Photo: Hackley Hall, c. 1920
Source: Museum Collection

The teachers and students raised the first money for the rebuilding of Hackley Hall, which now is a lovely brick building for the boys and was dedicated November 5, 1901, while Howland Hall is the girls' building.

"A Battleground School"
The Story of the Manassas Industrial School for Colored Youth, c. 1902

Photo Section

Howland Hall, Manassas Industrial School. Manassas, Va.

Breakfast for all students was at 8:00 A.M. in Howland Hall. The cook, Mrs. Derry, lived over the kitchen with her two small girls. Classes began at 9:00 A.M.; dinner was at noon and supper was at 6:00 P.M.

J. Harold Nickens, Sr., Oral History Interview

Photo: Howland Hall, c. 1920
Source: Museum Collection

The place is elevated and healthful, and surrounded by picturesque scenery. Free from the seductive influences of a city, this school offers a rare opportunity to those desirous of placing their children under elevating and purifying influences.

1902-03 Catalog

Photo: MIS campus, c. 1925
Source: Museum Collection

Photo Section

It is a beautiful brick structure with the Library, offices of the Principal and Treasurer, the Domestic Science and Dressmaking Departments and ample lavatories on the first floor. On the second floor are the well-lighted and well-ventilated class rooms of the Academic Department. The Assembly Hall is on the third floor.

1914 Catalog

Photo: Carnegie Building (1914 Catalog)
Source: The Library of Virginia

So important is the whole problem of a healthful and happy home life among our people that the school attaches particular importance to cooking and domestic science.

1912-13 Catalog

Photo: Domestic Science Dining Room, c. 1911
Source: Gift of Jennie Dean Club

Photo Section

The work in sewing covers a period of four years, the primary course teaching the use of thread, thimble, needle, and giving instruction in such work as would come under the head of plain sewing. The advanced course covers drafting, cutting and fitting, trimming, and fashionable dressmaking.

1908-09 Catalog

Photo: Sewing class (1914 Catalog)
Source: The Library of Virginia

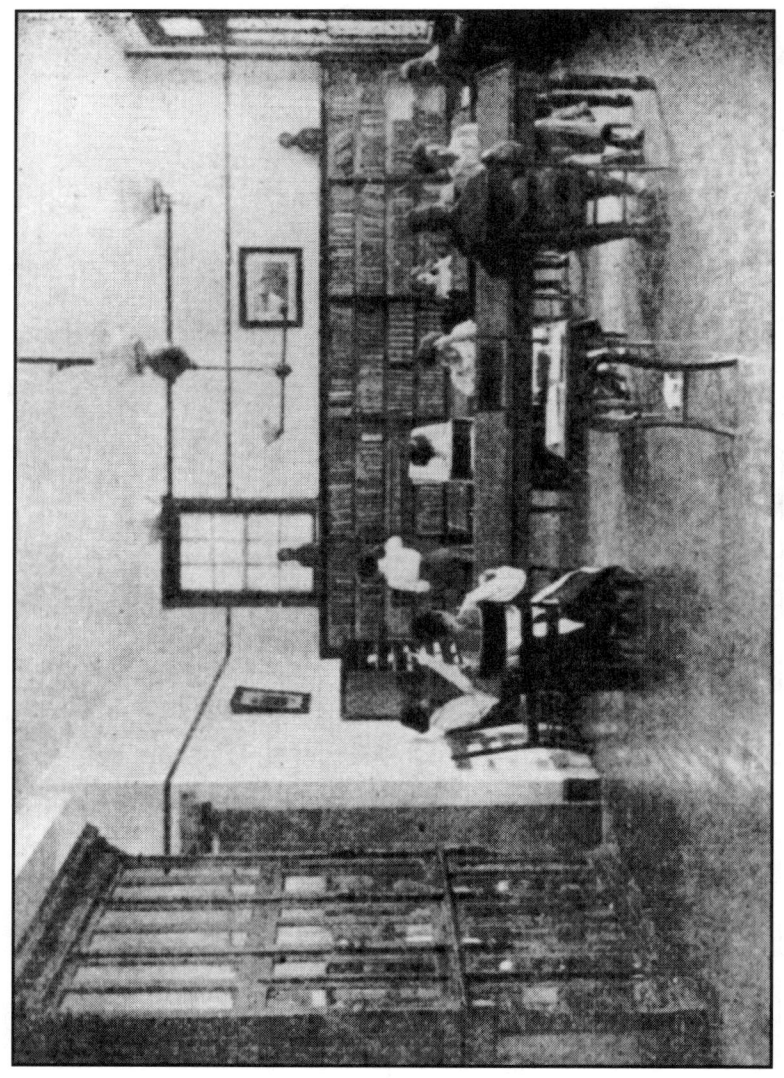

Of the 653 private and higher schools described in this report, only 27 are known to have a collection of books that on the most liberal interpretation could be called a library (Manassas is one of them).

1916 Federal Bureau of Education Report on Negro Education

Photo: Library (1914 Catalog)
Source: The Library of Virginia

Photo Section

The boys have a well-organized Athletic Association and engage in football, baseball, basketball, tennis and other forms of practicable out-of-door sports. The various teams play each season a limited number of games at other schools.

1915-16 Catalog

Photo: Football team (1915 Catalog)
Source: Gift of Rosa Farquhar

Not many rules are laid down, but whether in the recitation, in the shop, or in the field, at every point of the school life, the aim is to establish in the student body the habit of respectful obedience to authority, of courtesy, of faithful application to duty, of regulating conduct by high moral principles, and of confidence and pride in the race.

1915-16 Catalog

Photo: Glee Club (1915 Catalog)
Source: Gift of Rosa Farquhar

Photo Section

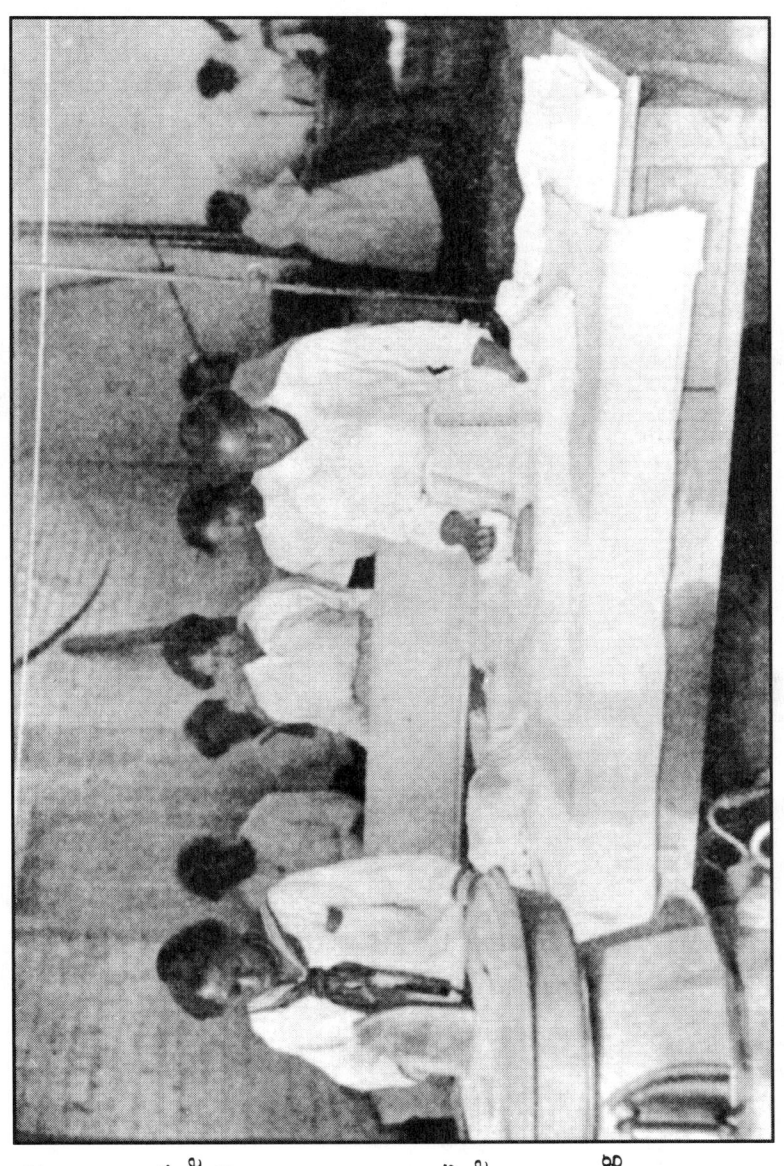

Every line of activity that aids in raising the standard of civilization ought to receive the fullest attention possible. A thoughtful study of the home will reveal the fact that it occupies a very important place in the field of social uplift. A thorough knowledge of the principles of the home and skill in applying these principles to the actual life itself are essential to the much desired social development.

1915-16 Catalog

Photo: Ironing class (1915 Catalog)
Source: Gift of Rosa Farquhar

We were considered the National High School Colored Relay Champions of America. We brought many trophies and honors to dear old M.I.S.

Dr. William Waddell, DMV
Oral History Interview

Photo: Track team c. 1927
Source: Gift of Jennie Dean Club

In athletics, the teams did very well. Competition was difficult to locate because of the paucity of colored high schools. M.I.S. competed in baseball, football and track against schools in D.C., Norfolk, Harper's Ferry, Baltimore and Bowie.

J. Harold Nickens, Sr.
Oral History Interview

Photo: Football team c. 1927
Source: Gift of B. Oswald Robinson
(Donor pictured in middle row, third from left)

Manassas Industrial School was a school where you really learned the value of being a person.

Louise Smith Brown, Oral History Interview

Photo: Leon Henderson (left) and Harold Nickens, Class of 1929
Source: Elizabeth Nickens

Photo Section

The buildings were around a tree-lined cinder-coated oval driveway with a well kept lawn with shrubs, flowers and walkways. A gazebo containing a drinking fountain was located in front of the main structure–Carnegie Hall.

J. Harold Nickens, Sr. Oral History Interview

Photo: William Wright, c. 1939-42
Source: James Knox

*In years to come,
And years to go
You will always know,
We'll think of you,
Manassas Dear,
And always love you so.*

1954 Class Song

Photo: Regional High School Christmas Events, 1953
Source: Museum Collection

Photo Section

I can recall the beautiful campus we had and the boys and girls would stroll on the campus and sit around.

Hilda Alexander Hicks
Oral History Interview

Photo: Carnegie Building, c. 1953
Source: Museum Collection

*The time has come,
Manassas dear,
When our paths
must part,
Memories of you
forever
Will be engraved
within our hearts.*

1954 Class Song

Photo: Regional High School Graduates, 1955
Source: Museum Collection

Photo Section

Although the years have swiftly passed
Our memories will always last,
For to us you are unforgettable
And not a moment here is regretable.

1952 Class Poem

Photo: Cheerleaders, 1953
Front (left to right): Messrs. Harrod and Monroe
Back (left to right): Misses Corum, Smith, Richards, Vaughn, Dyer, Brown, Thompson and Jones.
Source: Museum Collection

Photo: Jennie Dean High and Elementary School, c. 1960
Source: Gloria Bennett-Jones

The new Jennie Dean High School, a dream that took place in 1894 has been fulfilled in 1960. The new facilities, the volume-filled library, inviting classrooms, spacious gymnasium and the beautiful cafeteria and auditorium are open for your use.

1960 Jay Dee School Yearbook

Photo Section 119

What she sacrificed for and accomplished in Northern Virginia will remain a vital force for many generations to come . . . .

Undaunted Faith

Photo: Students and Faculty of Dean Elementary, Spring 1994
Source: Museum Collection

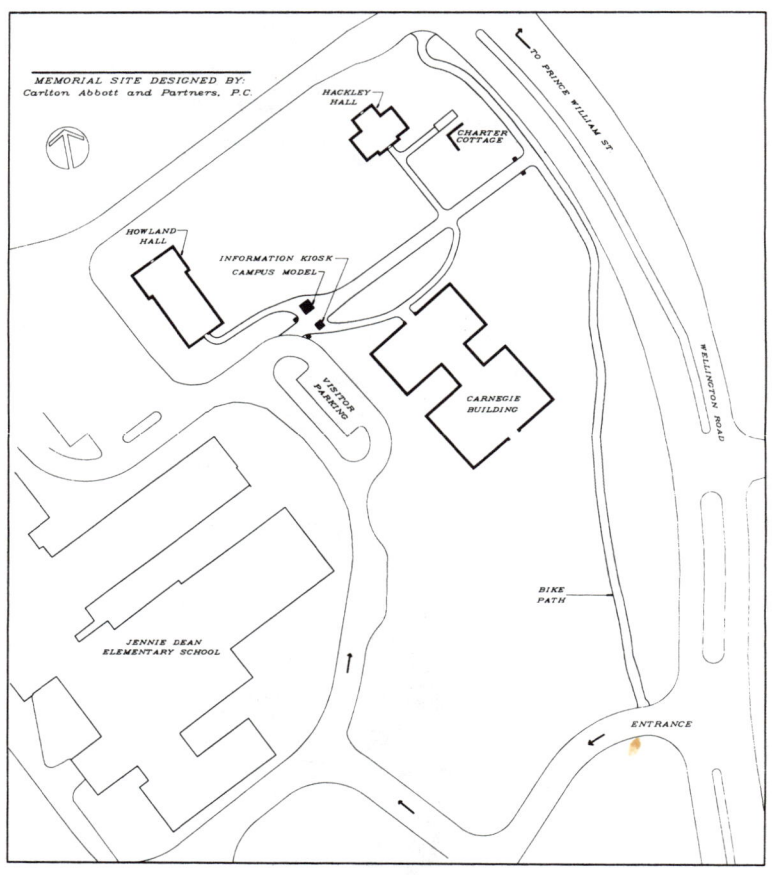

*It seems quite fitting, therefore, that a Jennie Dean Memorial
... should be erected on the school grounds with tablets ...
giving a history of her life and works.*
                        Jane E. Thompson
                        Manassas Journal, May 16, 1918

Map: MIS/Dean Memorial
Source: Carlton Abbott and Partners

Epilogue

By Laura A. Peake
and
Scott H. Harris

Epilogue

Jennie Dean's success in founding and nurturing the Manassas Industrial School would be considered a significant accomplishment for any person. The fact that she formed a bi-racial base of local support for the school in the late 19th century is a testament to her diplomatic skill. The fact that she obtained large sums of money for the school from northern philanthropists demonstrates her powers of persuasion. The fact that Jennie Dean did all of these things and more as an African-American ex-slave with little formal education illustrates her vision and perseverance.

As Dr. Lewis' biography of her vividly shows, Jennie Dean was not an ordinary woman. Various factors in her life imparted a determination and vision that few of her contemporaries could equal. She did not use these traits to benefit herself but rather to help other African-Americans in their quest for education, pride in accomplishment, and social responsibility. Miss Dean used her talents to establish a school "ultimately and primarily to improve the moral and intellectual condition of the youth placed under its care and influence," to quote from its 1893 Charter. Academic preparation was valued equally with vocational training. The charter further states that the students would receive "such instructions in the common English Branches, the Mechanical Arts and Trades in farming, housework, needle work, and other occupations . . . that shall be practicable and also useful in enabling the said youth to earn a livelihood."[1]

Jennie Dean's own schooling was rudimentary at best, a consequence of the legacy of slavery and the burdens of Jim Crow segregation. Despite this deprivation, or perhaps more accurately *because* of it, she was inspired to create a place of learning for her people. As a devout Christian she may well have drawn a parallel between the spiritual nature of her mission and that of Jesus Christ: "I must be about my Father's business." Without such firmness of purpose, the Manassas Industrial School might never have come into being.

The school at Manassas was not the only industrial school or educational institution for African-Americans in the Commonwealth of Virginia, however it did have many unique qualities. A Federal Bureau of Education report from 1916 lists 37 private and higher education schools for blacks. There were also approximately 50 small denominational and special institutions in the state that educated African-Americans. The size, classwork, industrial training, educational level, and ownership varied greatly from school to school. Public high schools for blacks existed in cities such as Lynchburg, Petersburg, Richmond, Norfolk, and Danville. Since the state government allocated only a small percentage of its educational funding for use in teaching African-Americans, there were more private institutions than public ones educating these students. A map of Virginia included in the 1916 report shows the more important private schools for African-Americans, including the Manassas Industrial School.[2]

Examination of the 37 Virginia schools reveals that only three were founded by women. Thirteen offered little or no industrial training, while the same number received some or all of their funding from public sources. Twenty-two of the 24 private schools that did not rely on public funding were affiliated with and/or run by religious organizations. The Manassas Industrial School for Colored Youth and the Franklin Normal and Industrial Institute in Southampton County were the only two private schools without a religious affiliation. Both of these schools were also founded by black women–Jennie Dean and Mrs. D.I. Hayden, respectively. The Manassas Industrial School, while not necessarily unique in Virginia or the South, did stand alone as the only school of its kind in Northern Virginia. As both a private and later a public institution, it remained the only source of a secondary level education for blacks in Northern Virginia until the era of desegregation. The closest school shown on the 1916 map was in Spotsylvania County (it was, however, significantly smaller). Henrico and Powhatan counties were the nearest counties that had schools of a comparable nature and both were over 75 miles south of Manassas.

The importance of the Manassas Industrial School was acknowledged by no less a personage than the President of the United States when Jennie Dean and a group of students visited the White House on February 14, 1906. Theodore Roosevelt praised the school and its aims: "Of course, Miss Dean, the good that comes with any such school as this is increased tenfold when the school is founded, as you founded this, and as Mr. Washington founded Tuskegee, by a colored man or colored woman to help the colored boys and colored girls of to-day to make the best type of self-respecting, self-supporting American citizens of the future."[3] This presidential commendation came five years after Roosevelt startled the nation by inviting Booker T. Washington to the White House for a similar meeting.

By the early 1940s, when Stephen Johnson Lewis ended his narrative of Jennie Dean's life and legacy, the Manassas Industrial School had entered a critical period of transition. The internal dissent and mounting financial burdens that had characterized the history of the school in the 1920s threatened to overwhelm the institution as the 1930s drew to a close. Salvation for the Manassas Industrial School came in the form of a new mode of ownership and operation as a regional high school for African-Americans in Northern Virginia.

Following much negotiation between officials of the school and surrounding counties, ownership of the Manassas Industrial School was transferred to the counties of Prince William, Fairfax, and Fauquier in 1938, thereby creating Manassas Regional High School. The three jurisdictions agreed to jointly administer the facility and assume all debts incurred during private operation, a sum of some $16,000. Under this arrangement, black students from the three "owning" counties and other localities received secondary instruction in academic and vocational subjects. The emphasis on agricultural training and production that had been a hallmark since classes started in 1894 was retained and strengthened, while a more vigorous academic curriculum was adopted.

In addition to Prince William, Fairfax, and Fauquier, students came to Manassas Regional High School from the counties of Arlington, Page, Rappahannock, Shenandoah, and Warren, as well as Ft. Belvoir, Falls Church, and other municipalities. During this period (1938-1953) the Manassas Regional High School was the only secondary school for people of color in Northern Virginia.[4] By combining the resources of the participating jurisdictions, the school was once again able to inculcate the values and instruction so cherished by Jennie Dean to an even greater number of children.

While the regional period brought stability and renewed life for the school at Manassas, it was vexed from the start by a fundamental obstacle–distance. Residency on the campus was limited by both physical space and funding, forcing much of the student population to commute. Some traveling from the farthest counties endured round trips of up to 150 miles each day. Anna E. Ferguson-Corbett, a student at the school from 1938-1942, recounts her commuting experience: "I lived in Gum Springs and we rode the bus to Manassas every day for four years, and also I will always be grateful to Mr. Ben Holland for driving the bus. It was a voluntary commitment on his part; he did not receive any salary. He knew we did not have any other school to go to so he gave his time so that we could get an education . . ."[5] Parental concerns were somewhat alleviated by the strong sense of purpose and caring attitude fostered by the school administration, faculty, and student body. Indeed, the Regional High School was able to more fully develop both the academic curriculum and extracurricular opportunities for students than had been possible over the preceding 45 years. However, the logistics of long-distance travel were an ever-present problem that ultimately led to a breakdown of the regional operation.

In 1953 Fauquier County became the first "owning" county to leave the fold. Distance and a desire of African-American residents of the county to have their children's school under more direct control were the major factors that led to the founding of W.C. Taylor High School (named

Epilogue

for a former Manassas Industrial School principal) in Warrenton. Fairfax County opened Luther P. Jackson High School in Merrifield the following year, causing another exodus of students from Manassas. Thus by 1954 Prince William County became the sole owner of the Regional High School, which continued to accept students from additional communities. Warren County continued to subsidize students who boarded at the Regional High School. Yet other events of that year signaled the beginning of the end of not only the regional concept, but of segregated education as well.

In May, 1954 the U.S. Supreme Court's landmark *Brown vs. Board of Education of Topeka, Kansas* decision mandated integration for all public schools in the nation. It was Virginia's sad fate to enter at this time a period of "massive resistance" to court-ordered desegregation, as the state political organization headed by U.S. Senator Harry F. Byrd sought to delay or subvert integration. Several counties and cities in the Commonwealth shut down their public schools rather than comply with the Supreme Court ruling. Warren County High School closed in 1958 as a protest against integration. When it reopened with very few white students in January, 1959 some blacks attended while others continued to receive instruction at the Regional High School until the end of the school year. The County pledged to build an all-black high school if a minimum of 100 African-American students were of high school age. Therefore, Criser High School in Front Royal was planned as an all-black school. However, by the time it opened in 1960 it was integrated. These events ended the attendance of African-Americans from Warren County at Manassas Regional High School. As the other contributing localities gradually integrated their schools, the focus of Manassas Regional High School narrowed to that of Prince William students only by 1959.[6]

In 1957 Prince William County authorized construction of a combined high and elementary school for blacks adjacent to the original Industrial School campus. Jennie Dean High and Elementary School opened in 1959 to serve the African-American youth of the area as demolition of the original buildings began. Although passage of the Civil Rights Act of 1964 accelerated the process of integration, it was not until 1966 that Jennie Dean was used for both black and white students. When Manassas was transformed from a town into a city in 1975 it paid Prince William County to operate schools for City children, pending establishment of a Manassas school system. This occurred in 1977, and the City assumed ownership of Dean in that year. Since Osbourn High School already existed to serve secondary students, Dean was reorganized as a middle school. Metz Junior High School's opening in 1990 resulted in the current incarnation, Jennie Dean Elementary School.

The original Manassas Industrial School buildings were gradually torn down during the 1960s, with the exception of the Black Cottage, a frame building constructed as a student project around 1914. This structure was moved off the school site to nearby Jefferson Street and became a private residence–the only building of the Manassas Industrial School that survives today. Entrance gates were erected over the years by alumni of the school as were historical markers commemorating Carnegie, Howland, and Hackley Halls and the Charter Cottage. Realignment of Wellington Road in 1988 eradicated part of the Charter Cottage site following archaeological excavations that documented building remains and recovered artifacts.

The public controversy which attended the Wellington Road project served to focus attention on the importance of the Manassas Industrial School as an historical and educational resource, as well as dramatize its vulnerability. The site was incorporated into The Manassas Museum System in 1989, and planning began for the Manassas Industrial School/Jennie Dean Memorial. With the cooperation and support of the City of Manassas School Board, the City Council appropriated planning funds for the project and a public hearing was held in 1989 to solicit community opinion and support. The architectural firm of Carlton Abbott and Partners of Williamsburg, Virginia, the Manassas Society for the Preservation of Black Heritage, the Manassas Historical Committee, and the Museum staff began working together to create a conceptual plan. A second public meeting in March, 1992 brought out some 120 people who voiced support for the project. This was followed by City Council approval of a conceptual plan on April 27, 1992.

Epilogue

The MIS/Dean Memorial project is divided into two phases. Phase I entails outlines of the foundations of three original campus buildings, new historical markers and trails, an information kiosk, a scale model of the campus, and possibly a sculpture honoring Jennie Dean. Phase II envisions a replica of the school's horse barn as the stage of an amphitheater for the performing arts located in a replicated grove of trees once used for commencement exercises. The estimated costs for the project are $350,000 for Phase I and $650,000 for Phase II. At the time of this volume's publication the Phase I goal had been met (a list of project donors is included as a separate section of this publication). The Memorial site was placed on the Virginia and National Registers of Historic Places in May and August, 1994, respectively. Public opening of the Manassas Industrial School/Jennie Dean Memorial is slated for the Spring of 1995.

In creating this memorial to Jennie Dean and the school she founded, the greater Manassas community recognizes and honors the extraordinary efforts of a visionary African-American woman. Rising above the burdens imposed on her gender and race by 19th-century American society, Miss Dean devoted herself to establishing a school that would provide both practical training and a philosophy of self-improvement and responsibility.

Frederick Douglass concluded his speech at the dedication of the Manassas Industrial School for Colored Youth on September 3, 1894 with the following statement:

> *Imitate the example of the brave mariner who, amid clouds and darkness, amid hail, rain and storm bolts, battles his way against all that the sea opposes to his progress, and you will reach the goal of your noble ambition in safety.*[7]

This analogy amply describes the story of Jennie Dean and the school that was her dream. Hopefully many more brave mariners have reached their goal in safety as a result of the training and education received at the Manassas Industrial School for Colored Youth and its successors. Whether public or private, high school or elementary, black or white, the site of the school has been imbued with the spirit of Jennie Dean. Students of many races are now edu-

spirit of Jennie Dean. Students of many races are now educated at a place that for over a century has been witness to learning and achievement. Many of the fundamental concepts articulated by Miss Dean in the formation of the Manassas Industrial School have remained constant throughout its history. Jennie Dean herself continues to serve as an example of what one can accomplish in life with determination and a sense of purpose. She was indeed a person of Undaunted Faith.

Notes

[1] Prince William County Charter Book, I, pp. 36-37.
[2] Thomas Jesse Jones, *Negro Education: A Study of the Private and Higher Schools for Colored People in the United States*. 2 vols. U.S. Department of the Interior, Bureau of Education, Bulletins 38 and 39. (Washington, D.C.: U.S. Government Printing Office, 1917).
[3] Herman Hagedorn, ed., *The Works of Theodore Roosevelt*, 20 vols. (New York: P.F. Collier & Son, 1926), Vol. 5, p. 677.
[4] Commodore Bennett, "View of the Mountain: Jennie Dean of Virginia" (Unpublished manuscript). Commodore Bennett taught at the Manassas Industrial School and was later principal of Manassas Regional High School and Jennie Dean High and Elementary School. In the 1970s Dr. Bennett compiled an evaluation of the Manassas Industrial School in its various incarnations entitled "View of the Mountain." This work, while not a formal history, provided valuable insights to the authors of this Epilogue.
[5] Personal correspondence of Anna E. Ferguson-Corbett to The Manassas Museum, September 20, 1993.
[6] Personal correspondence of Briley Morrison to The Manassas Museum, April 20, 1994. Mr. Morrison, a retired educator, provided his observations regarding the process of integration in Warren County schools in the 1960s.
[7] John W. Blassingame and John R. McKivigan, eds. *The Frederick Douglass Papers*, Volume V, (New Haven and London:Yale University Press, 1979), p. 629.

Index

A

Aimee, Aunt 5
Alexander, Dr. Fred M. 84
Alexandria, Virginia 34, 69
All Souls Church 33
Anderson, Mr. L.I. 31
Apostle Paul 24
Arlington, Virginia 126
Athletic Association 107
Ayers, Henry 31

B

Bailey, Mrs. Ella Dean 5
Bailey, Rev. L.H. 6, 24, 31
Baker, Mr. H.E. 25
Baker, Henry F. 49
Baptist Association of Northern Virginia 62
Baptist Minister's Conference of Washington, D.C. 84
Barber, Susan 27
Barnes, Rev. William H. 43, 49, 75, 83, 88
Barton, Clara 45
Battle, Gordon 66
Bell, Elder 31
Bennet, Henry 5
Berea College 35, 50, 51
Berry, Henry 27
Berry, Mrs. G. 27
Berwind, John E. 68, 98
Berwind Hospital 68, 98
Bethune, Mary McLeod 9, 10, 46
Black Cottage 128
Blue Ridge Mountains 69
Board of Managers 25
Board of Trustees 62, 68, 73, 77, 84

Boston   25, 26, 27, 33, 34, 35, 43, 45, 61
Bradford, James H.   49
Bradford, Rev.   28
Brenton, Hampton   24
Brentsville, Virginia   69
Brooks, Bishop Phillip   26, 37
Brower, Dr. C.F.   31
Brown, Louise Smith   112
Brown, Miss   117
Brown School   53
Brown vs. Board of Education of Topeka, Kansas   127
Bull Run   6, 21, 27
Bull Run Church   31
Burton, Mrs. Harrison   34
Byrd, U.S. Senator Harry F.   127

C

Calvary Chapel, Catharpin, Virginia   14
Carlton Abbott and Partners   128
Carnegie, Andrew   62, 63
Carnegie Building   78, 103, 113, 115, 128
Catharpin, Virginia   59, 62, 66, 14, 25, 31
Chaney   1, 14
Chapman, Martha   27
Charter Cottage   66, 30, 91, 128
Cheney Institute   67
Chicago   61
City of Manassas School Board   128
Civil Rights Act of 1964   127
Civil War   xxiv, 9
Clarendon Street Baptist Church   26
Clarkson, Dr. H.M.   25, 28, 44
Clemens, Dr. Elijah P.   30, 44, 46, 50
Clemons, Mrs.   30
Cleveland   61
Clifford, John   44
Collier, Rev.   33
Congregational Bible Missions School   24
Conklin, Virginia   26, 27, 31
Conner, Abraham   45
Cook, Miss M.B.   34
Corum, Miss   117
County High School   83
County Supervisors of Prince William County   83
Creditt, Rev.   28
Criser High School   127
Culpeper, Virginia   29

Curry, Dr. J.L.M. 45
Cushing Family 5
Cushing, 'Squire' 25, 31

D

Danville, Virginia 124
Darling, Mrs. L.A. 34, 35
Davis, Mrs. Bancroft 35
Dean, Annie 5
Dean, Charles 5
Dean, Ella (Ella Dean Bailey) 23
Dean-Divers Chapel, Prince William County, Virginia 14
Dean, Mrs. Charles 27
Dean, Jane Serepta (full name of Jennie Dean) 5
Deans, Jeannie 63
Decatur, William J. 67, 69
Department of the Interior 45
Dodge, Mr. H.P. 34
Dodge, Mrs. E.B. 45
Domestic Science Dining Room 104
Doolittle, Lucy S. 49
Douglas, Mrs. F. 27
Douglass, Frederick xix, 7, 28, 44, 129
Dudley, Col. 26
Dudley, George 74, 79, 80, 83
Dyer, Miss 117

E

Edelin, Mr. A.B. 74
Elliot, Rev. 34
Elliott, Nelson 27

F

Fairfax County, Virginia 69, 83, 84, 87, 125, 127
Falls Church, Virginia 126
Fauquier County, Virginia 44, 69, 83, 84, 87, 125, 126
Federal Bureau of Education 106, 124
Ferguson-Corbett, Anna E. 126
"Fighting Years" 63, 74
First Congregational Church 25
Florida 9
Franklin Normal and Industrial Institute 124
Free, John 27
Front Royal, Virginia 127
Ft. Belvoir, Virginia 126

G

Gaines, Judge 25
Gainesville, Virginia 27
Garrison, William Lloyd 50
General Assembly 70
Gilliam, Henry 27
Glee Club 108
Gloucester Court House, Virginia 74
Gordon, Dr. A.J. 26, 34
Grace Church 33
Grant, Rev. 33
Green, John 27
Greer, Rev. 33
Griffin, William 27
Gum Springs, Virginia 126

H

Hackley Hall 15, 34, 35, 100, 128
Hackley, Mrs. C.B. (Frances) 34, 76
Hale, Dr. Edward Everett 26, 34, 37, 43, 45
Hale, Mrs. L.A. 34, 35
Hampton Brenton Farm 18
Hampton Institute 14, 35, 42
Harris, Anthony 27
Harris, Mrs. F. 27
Harris, William T. 45
Harrisburg, Pennsylvania 71
Harrod, Mr. 117
Harvard College 60
Hawkins, Charlotte Brown 9
Hayden, Mrs. D.I. 124
Haydon, Richard C. 80, 84, 85, 88
Haymarket, Virginia 25
Henderson, Leon 112
Henderson, Rev. J.D. 31
Henderson, Rev. D.G. 23, 62
Henderson Institute 83
Henderson, North Carolina 83
Henrico County, Virginia 125
Hicks, Hilda Alexander 115
Hill, Dr. Leslie Pinckney 59, 60, 61, 62, 66, 69
Holland, Ben 126
Horse Barn 95
House of Representatives 44
Howard University 25, 35
Howe, Edward D. 67, 68, 69, 70, 71, 74

Howland Hall   28, 30, 31, 33, 34, 35, 45, 100, 101, 128
Howland, Emily   28, 45, 76
Howland, Mrs. Judge   34
Huntington, Rev.   33
Hunton, Gen. Eppa   45

I

Iden, Dr. Benjamin   68

J

Jackson, William   27
Jefferson, Thomas   30
Jennie Dean Elementary School   118, 128
Jennie Dean High and Elementary School   118, 127
Jennie Dean High School   118
Jennie Dean Memorial   120
Jennie Dean Memorial Auditorium-Gymnasium   88
"Jennie Dean's Rules for Good Behavior Among her People"   10
Jim Crow   123
Johnson, John   24, 25, 27
Johnson, Samuel W.   35
Jones, Miss   117

K

Kettle Run School   69
King, Dr. B.P.M.   25

L

Langhorne, Mrs.   28
Langston, John M.   25
Lewis, Miss Eva P.   68
Lewis family   35
Lewis, Landonia   27, 30
Lewis, Mr. Roscoe C.   35, 80
Lewis, Stephen Johnson   75, 123, 125
Lewis, William   27
Lincoln, Abraham   xix, 7
Lipscomb, William E.   44
Literary Fund   85
Loudoun County, Virginia   14
Loving, Bessie E.   35, 53
Luther P. Jackson High School   127
Lynchburg, Virginia   124

M

Manassas City Council 128
Manassas Historical Committee 128
Manassas Industrial School/Jennie Dean Memorial 120, 128, 129
Manassas Junction 17
Manassas Museum System 128
Manassas Regional High School 30, 53, 77, 84, 87, 125, 126, 127
Manassas Society for the Preservation of Black Heritage 128
Manly School 1
Marion, Massachusetts 25
Marshall, Rev. L.L. 29
Martin, Mary Dean 5
Massey, John E. 45
Mays, George 60, 69
Meredith, Congressman E.E. 25, 44
Merrifield, Virginia 127
Merriwether, James H. 49
Metcalfe, Mr. 31
Metz Junior High School 128
Mildred (Jennie Dean's grandmother) 5
Miller, Kelley 66
Monroe, Mr. 117
Montgomery, Emma V. 34, 49
Montgomery, Prof. Henry P. 25, 30, 33, 44, 49
Morton, Fred D. 67, 69
Mrs. Bancroft Davis' Cooking School (D.C.) 35
Mt. Calvary Church 31
Mussey, Gen. 25
Mussey, Mrs. Ellen S. 45, 51
'My Country Tis of Thee' 28

N

National High School Colored Relay Champions 110
National Register of Historic Places 129
New England 22
New York 25, 33, 34, 35, 45, 50, 61
New York City 22
New York Evening Post 5, 13, 50
Newman, Dr. 25
Newman family 5
Nichol, Charles E. 44
Nickens, Harold (J. Harold Nickens, Sr.) 101, 111, 112, 113
Nineteenth Street Baptist Church xxiii
Norfolk, Virginia 124
North Carolina 9
Northern Virginia Baptist Association xx

O

Occoquan, Virginia 24
Old South Church 26
Osbourn High School 128
Osgood, Miss 35

P

Page County, Virginia 126
Patman, Thomas 31
Peabody Fund 45
Pennsylvania 67
Pennsylvania State Teacher's College 67
Peters, John 27
Petersburg, Virginia 124
Polen, Mr. J.D. 31
Potter, Bishop 33
Powhatan County, Virginia 125
Prince William County 25, 49, 53, 68, 69, 80, 83, 87, 93, 125, 127, 128
Prince William County Schools 44
Prosperity Chapel, Loudoun County, Virginia 14, 31

R

Randolph Macon College 45
Rankin, Dr. 25
Rappahannock County, Virginia 69, 87, 126
Red Cross 45
Regional Board 77
Richards, Miss 117
Richmond, Virginia 124
Robinson, B. Oswald 111
Robinson, Bladen 27
Robinson, Tasker 27
Roosevelt, Theodore 125
Round, George C. 25, 43, 44, 45, 49
Ruben (Jennie Dean's grandfather) 5

S

Sampson, George W. 69, 74
Sanders, Mr. F.H. 31
Savage, Dr. J.M. 26
Scott, Sir Walter 63
Shellington, John 23, 27
Shenandoah County, Virginia 126
Sherwood, New York 28
Shippen, Rush H. 49

Shippens, Dr. R.R. 25
Sidney, Dr. B. Hall 84
Slater, William A. 45
Slater Fund 45
Smith, Dr. William W. 45
Smith, Hoke 45
Smith, Miss 117
"Social Graces and the Negro" 9
Southampton County, Virginia 124
Southern Railway 17
Spotsylvania County, Virginia 124
State Board of Education 84, 86
State Department of Education 85, 86
State Superintendent of Public Instruction 84
State Supervisor of Negro Schools 84
Stokes, Sallie 27
Strasburg Branch, Southern Railway 17
Sudley Springs, Virginia 3, 5, 6, 27, 30, 31

T

Taylor, Prof. William C. 51, 60, 74
"The Beginning of The Manassas Industrial School For Colored Youth and Its Growth" 21
"Third Battle of Manassas" 21
Thompson, Jane E. 17, 23, 25, 26, 28, 43, 44, 49, 56, 62, 117, 120
Thompson, Mrs. Josephine 35
Thornton, Mr. J.B.T. 45
Thoroughfare Gap 17, 23, 24, 30
Three-County Board 87
Topsy 7
Tuskegee 14, 42, 55, 60, 125
Tyler, Capt. R.H. 25, 28, 44

U

U.S. Supreme Court 127
Union University 79

V

Vaughn, Miss 117
Vernon, Mary E. (Mary Vernon Ware) 30, 35, 53
Villard, Oswald Garrison 5, 6, 7, 13, 14, 18, 41, 46, 50, 51, 55, 60, 61, 62, 63, 73, 74, 75
Virginia, Commonwealth of 43, 124
Virginia Register of Historic Places 129

W

W.C. Taylor High School 126
Waddell, Dr. William 99, 110
Walker, Mr. T.C. 74, 76
Waring, Rev. Henry H. 34, 49
Warren County, Virginia 87, 126, 127
Warrenton, Virginia 25, 127
Washington, Booker T. xix, 7, 10, 55, 85, 125
Washington, D.C. xxiii, xxiv, 6, 7, 14, 25, 26, 28, 35, 44, 45, 50, 53, 54
Washington, David 27
Wayland Seminary 6, 25
Wellington, Virginia 27
White House 125
White, John W. 35, 53, 54
White, Bessie Loving 53
Whitman, Mrs. M.C. 26, 27
Wilcox, Mrs. 26
Williams, Dr. John D. 76, 77, 79, 80
Williams, Rev. Marshall D. 24, 25, 27, 33, 44, 49, 77
Williams, Emma Lee 69, 74
Williams, Mrs. M.D. 27, 30
Williamsburg, Virginia 128
"Wings Over Jordan." 9
Women's Suffrage Convention 28
Woodford, Prof. E.H. 35, 50, 51, 60
World War I 64, 73
Wright, Carroll D. 49, 50
Wright, William 113

Bibliography

Anderson, James D. *The Education of Blacks in the South, 1860-1935.* Chapel Hill: The University of North Carolina Press, 1988.

Bennett, Commodore N. "View of the Mountain: Jennie Dean of Virginia," (unpublished manuscript).

Dean, Jennie. *The Beginning of the Manassas Industrial School for Colored Youth and Its Growth, 1888-1900.* n.p., 1900.

Jones, Thomas Jesse. *Negro Education: A Study of the Private and Higher Schools for Colored People in the United States.* 2 vols. U.S. Department of the Interior, Bureau of Education, Bulletins 38 and 39. Washington, D.C.: U.S. Government Printing Office, 1917.

Manassas Industrial School. *A Battleground School: A Colored Woman's Work in Uplifting Negro Boys and Girls.* n.p., n.d.

_____. *The Manassas Industrial School for Colored Youth Located at Manassas, Virginia.* Manassas, Virginia: Manassas Industrial School for Colored Youth, 1902-03.

_____. *Financial Statement and Donors' List.* Manassas, Virginia: Manassas Industrial School for Colored Youth, 1904-05.

_____. *Financial Report, Donors' List and Statement of Current Needs.* Manassas, Virginia: Manassas Industrial School for the Training of Colored Youth, 1907.

_____. *The Manassas Industrial School for the Training of Colored Youth.* Manassas, Virginia, Manassas Industrial School for the Training of Colored Youth, 1908-09.

_____. *Financial Report, Donors' List and Statement of Current Needs.* Manassas, Virginia: Manassas Industrial School for the Training of Colored Youth, 1909.

_____. *Financial Report, Donors' List and Statement of Current Needs.* Manassas, Virginia: Manassas Industrial School for the Training of Colored Youth, 1910.

_____. *Summer School for Teachers and Students.* Manassas, Virginia: Manassas Industrial School for Colored Youth, 1911.

_____. *The Manassas Industrial School for the Training of Colored Youth.* Manassas, Virginia: Manassas Industrial School for the Training of Colored Youth, 1912-13.

_____. *The Manassas Summer School for Teachers and Students.* Manassas, Virginia: Manassas Industrial School, 1912.

_____. *The Manassas Summer School for Teachers and Students.* Manassas, Virginia: Manassas Industrial School, 1914.

_____. *The Manassas Industrial School for the Training of Colored Youth.* Manassas, Virginia: Manassas Industrial School for the Training of Colored Youth, 1914-15.

_____. *The Manassas Industrial School for the Training of Colored Youth.* Manassas, Virginia: Manassas Industrial School for the Training of Colored Youth, 1915-16.

_____. *Summer Session for Teachers.* Manassas, Virginia: Manassas Industrial School, 1916.

_____. *Summer Session for Teachers.* Manassas, Virginia: Manassas Industrial School, 1918.

_____. *The Manassas Industrial School Bulletin.* Manassas, Virginia: Manassas Industrial School, 1925.

_____. *Bulletin, Manassas Industrial School Summer School.* Manassas, Virginia: Manassas Industrial School, 1927.

_____. *Summer School Bulletin.* Manassas, Virginia: Manassas Industrial School, 1929.

Bibliography

———. *Summer School Bulletin.* Manassas, Virginia: Manassas Industrial School, 1930.

———. "Preliminary Annual High School Report." Manassas, Virginia, 1932-33.

———. "Final Annual High School Report." Manassas, Virginia, 1932-33.

———. "Preliminary Annual High School Report." Manassas, Virginia, 1933-34.

———. "Final Annual High School Report." Manassas, Virginia, 1933-34.

———. "Preliminary Annual High School Report." Manassas, Virginia, 1934-35.

———. "Final Annual High School Report." Manassas, Virginia, 1934-35.

———. "Preliminary Annual High School Report." Manassas, Virginia, 1935-36.

———. "Final Annual High School Report." Manassas, Virginia, 1935-36.

———. "Preliminary Annual High School Report." Manassas, Virginia, 1936-37.

———. "Final Annual High School Report." Manassas, Virginia, 1936-37.

———. "Preliminary Annual High School Report." Manassas, Virginia, 1937-38.

———. "Final Annual High School Report." Manassas, Virginia, 1937-38.

Manassas Museum. *Word From the Junction: The Manassas Museum News* 10(3), May-June 1992.

Mills, Charles A. *Echoes of Manassas.* Edited by Donald Wilson. Manassas, Virginia: Friends of the Manassas Museum, 1988.

Sanborn Map Company. *Insurance Map for Manassas, Virginia.* New York: Sanborn Map Company, 1912.

———. *Insurance Map for Manassas, Virginia.* New York: Sanborn Map Company, 1924.

_____. *Insurance Map for Manassas, Virginia.* New York: Sanborn Map Company, 1943.

Simmons, Catherine T. *Manassas, Virginia 1873-1973.* Edited by Douglas K. Harvey. Manassas, Virginia: The Manassas City Museum, 1986.

Thompson, Harry F. *"Survey of Manassas Industrial School, Manassas, Virginia by the Boston Insurance Company."* Manassas, Virginia, 1938.

Various archaeological reports which include information on the Manassas Industrial School site are on file at The Manassas Museum.

Donors to the Manassas Industrial School Jennie Dean Memorial Project

Donors

In Amounts of $100 or Greater

African-American Festival
   Foundation
Alpha Phi Alpha Fraternity, Inc.
   Xi Alpha Lambda Chapter
Alsop, Iris Hairston–
   Faculty Member, 1950-54
Alsop, Simon L.–
   Teacher & Asst. Principal, 1949-53
Anderson, Margaret E.
Arrington, Mr. & Mrs. Paul J.
Baptist Women's Convention of
   No. Va., Inc.
Barg, Hilda M.
Beard, Rose R.
Beautification Committee
Bennett-Jones, Gloria J.
Blayton, Benjamin B.
Bowers, Dr. Detine L.
Bowles, James C.–In memory of
   Cassie Warrington Bowles
Braxton, Carroll W. & Celestine S.
Brown, Mr. & Mrs. Edward L
Brown, Louise Smith
Buchanan, L.P.
Burrell, William H.
Burton, Dr. Judith Saunders
Butler, Dorothy C.–Class of 1944
   In loving memory of
   Howard Henry Butler (MIS 1941)
Carter, Olivia Addison
Cartwright, John & C.J.
Casey, Flora A.
Chantilly Baptist Church
Chapman, Charles S.
Churchill, Mr. & Mrs. Howard B.
   & Family
City of Manassas
Coalition of 100 Black Women, Inc.
   Northern Virginia Chapter
Coldwell, Louise G.
Cole, Samuel J. & Julia
Coleman, Mr. & Mrs. Edward A.
Commonwealth of Virginia
Conner, Mr. & Mrs. Edgar R., Jr.
Cooksey, Althea
Cooksey, Howard
County of Fairfax
Cox, Elvere
Dance, Kermit & Blanche & Family
Davis, Delores
Dean, Edward
Dean, Edwina Groeflin
Dean, Raymond Reginald, Jr.
Delisle Antiques
Dixon, Frank
Douglas, William H.
Ellis, Mrs. Mearita
Ellis, S. Gilbert
Fairfax Central Baptist
   Sunday School Union
Fincham, Russell M., Sr.
First A.M.E. Church of Manassas
First American Fireworks
First Baptist Church
Gerson, Mr. & Mrs. Maury
Gillum, Dr. & Mrs. Marvin L.
Gormes, Lucinda Brook
Gower, Dr. & Mrs. Arthur
Gregory, John & Angela
Grzejka, Councilman John
Gustin, Florence S.
Guy, Richard & Shirley
Halbert, Bertram
Hall, Sue
Harris, Julia Williams
Harrover, Ann R.
Harvey, Mr. & Mrs. Douglas K.
Heltzel Mortgage Corporation
Hempen, Ann, Mark & Jesse
Henley, Vernard W.

Henry, Gilbert
Historic Prince William
Holiday Sales
Hudspeth, Mrs. R.C.
Hughes, Gregory George
IBM
Independent Bank
Jackson, Ada Paige
Jackson, Clyde & Sandra
Jackson, Janice F.
Jenkins, Hon. John
Jennie Dean Elementary School–
  Staff, Faculty, and Students
Jerry's Lincoln Mercury
Johnson, Mrs. Gem
Johnson, Mrs. J. Benjamin
Jones Family: Wesley G., Lindsay R.,
  Louise J., George R., Audrey V.–
  In memory of
  Lindsay Robertson Jones, Jr. &
  Ruth Louise Washington Jones
Junior Women's Club of Manassas,
  Inc.
Kettlewell, Charles & Gail
Kline Memorials
Knight, Mary Ella Mitchell
Kuhn, Debby
Kye, Floyd C.
Lawrence, Mr. & Mrs. Stephen T.
LeKander, Mrs. Gilbert
Lewis, Cornelia B.
Lewis, Diane M.
Lewis, Marion E.
Light, Mrs. Belva Ellison
Light, Meredith
Little Union Baptist Church
Little Zion Baptist Church, Greenville
Lottier, Diane D.–Principal of
  Jennie Dean Elementary School
Luck Stone Corporation
Lyons, Mr. & Mrs. G. Keith
M.R.H.S. Class of '52 Reunion Club
Makell, William & Yvonne
Manassas Chrysler Plymouth
Manassas Ice and Fuel, Inc.
Manassas Museum Associates
Manassas Society for the Preservation
  of Black Heritage
McBryde Unger, Nancy
McCarron, Kay R.
McGolrick, Mr. & Mrs. J. Edward, Jr.
Merchant, Mrs. Mae S.
Merchant Tire

Mitchell, Paul W.
Mount Calvary Baptist Church
Mount Olive Baptist Church
  Rectortown
Mount Olive Baptist Church
  Garrisonville
Mount Pleasant Baptist Church
  Missionary Board
Multi-Group Industries, USA, Inc./
  Col. and Mrs. Ulysses X. White
Muse, Domily H.
Nash, Curtis & Betty
National Council of Negro Women
  Northern Virginia Section
NAVCOM Charities Foundation, Inc.
Nelson, Charles H., Jr., D.D.S.
Nia's Books and Things
19th Street Baptist Church
Norman Realty
O'Neill, Auston & Phyllis
O'Neill, Shirley F.
Oakrum Baptist Church
Oakshade Baptist Church
P.J.'s Pen
Pohl, Mr. Ronald K.
Powell, Alfred M.
Prince William County
Prince William County
  Historical Commission
Proctor, Emily Harris
R.C. Haydon Elementary School SCA
Rathke, Dr. & Mrs. Charles E..
Riley, Susie Toler–Class of 1912
Ringler, Lelia D.
Robertson, Merritt & Cynthia
Robinson, Rev. Dr. Clarence A.–
  Class of 1943
Seefeldt, Kathleen K.
Shaw, Ms. Eirea A,.–Teacher
  Social Studies/Art/Cosmetology
Sheppard, Marie E.
Slonim, Mr. & Mrs. Charles E.
Smith, Charles A.
Smith, Dorothy Lomax
Social Security Administration
  Dept. of Health & Human Services
Sprow, Mr. & Mrs. William A.
Sprunger, Cynthia D.
Stallworth, Eddie
Stine, Mr. & Mrs. Ronald C.
Taylor, Mr. & Mrs. Curtis
Taylor, Mrs. Odessa M.
Thornton, Col. & Mrs. C.R.

Donors

Timbers, Lydia Riley
Union, T.M.D. & C.
Waddell, Dr. William H.
Washington, G.E.
Weems Elementary School–
 Staff, Faculty, and Students
We, Us, and Them Club

Wellington Land Developers
Williams, Mr. & Mrs. Ulysses S.
Wilson, Mr. & Mrs. David E.
Wilson, Donald L.
Wilson, Gilmer & Frances
Women in Community Action
Yates, James L.